Northern Summer

Also by John Matthias

POETRY

Bucyrus   1970
Turns   1975
Crossing   1979
Batory & Lermontov   1980

TRANSLATIONS
(*with Göran Printz-Påhlson*)

Contemporary Swedish Poetry   1980
Jan Östergren: Rainmaker   1983

EDITIONS

23 Modern British Poets   1971
Five American Poets   1979
Introducing David Jones   1980

John Matthias

Northern Summer

NEW AND SELECTED POEMS 1963-1983

Swallow Press
Athens, Ohio

Library of Congress Cataloging in Publication Data

Matthias, John, 1941-
    Northern summer.

    I. Title.
PS3563.A858N6   1984   811'.54   83-18199
ISBN 0-8040-0852-3
ISBN 0-8040-0853-1 (pbk.)

CONTENTS

4 Translations, Imitations, Dedications

5 *from* Batory & Lermontov

6 New Poems

Foreword

Only "Swimming at Midnight" authenticates the first of my dates, having been written in California in 1963. The other poems in *Bucyrus* (1970) were written either in London during the academic year 1966-67, or in South Bend, Indiana during 1967-68. It has been difficult to make selections from *Bucyrus*. The one poem I can still be enthusiastic about from that early volume, "Poem in Three Parts", is some thirty pages long. Because I want to represent more recent long poems in the present book, I can only excerpt three sections from the one in *Bucyrus*: "Renaissance" (in *Bucyrus*, "Preface to 'Poem in Three Parts': Two"), "An Absence" (in *Bucyrus*, "Preface to 'Poem in Three Parts': One"), and the "Five Lyrics from 'Poem in Three Parts'" (the original parts *vii* to *xi* of Section Two). I have changed other titles of poems from this book, but I have left the texts alone. "Portrait, Room and Dream" has become "Triptych"; "Homicidal" and "Suicidal" have become "Diptych"; and "Alastor McGibbon" has become "Arzeno Kirkpatrick" (cf. the "Proem" to "The Mihail Lermontov Poems"). "Statement", also from *Bucyrus*, is printed at the end of the book with the bibliographical notes.

From *Turns* (1975), my first book to be published in England as well as America, I have selected liberally. Nearly all of the poems chosen were written in Suffolk or Cambridge between 1972 and 1974. *Crossing* (1979) continues the search for a sense of rootedness in a land not my own begun in *Turns*. Nearly all of the poems appearing in this section were written at Clare Hall, Cambridge during 1976-77. A section of translations, collaborations, dedications and imitations produced over a number of years divides "The Stefan Batory Poems" and selections from "The Mihail Lermontov Poems" from the shorter pieces that preceded them in *Crossing*. Although these two sea-going cycles concluded *Crossing*, they also appeared on their own in 1980 as *Batory & Lermontov*, a bilingual volume published in Sweden with Swedish translations by Göran Printz-Påhlson and Jan Östergren, and monotype illustrations by Douglas Kinsey. The "Batory Poems" were drafted while returning to America after a year in England on the Polish liner *Stefan Batory* during the final stages of the Watergate controversy in the summer of 1974; the "Lermontov Poems" were drafted two years later on a

7

Russian ship, the *Mihail Lermontov*, as I sailed to England again to take up residence for a year at Clare Hall. All but one of the "New Poems" in the concluding section have been written between 1980 and 1983. The title poem, "Northern Summer", was begun in Fife, Scotland, on the Wemyss Castle Estate in the summer of 1980 and finished three years later in the Cambridgeshire village of Trumpington. The middle parts were written in a cabin on Lake Michigan in 1982. (I should probably note, chiefly for American readers, that Wemyss is a monosyllabic word, pronounced *Weems*.)

Some readers, particularly those already acquainted with at least some of a poet's work, prefer to read a retrospective volume in reverse chronological order. I have no objection to the numbered chronological sections of the book being read in that order, provided that the individual poems making up each section are themselves read in the order in which they appear. I am almost tempted to ask the *new* reader to begin with section 2, the poems from *Turns*, where I begin to feel confident of whatever abilities I have.

Many acknowledgements are in order in addition to those listed in the notes at the end of the book. I wish to thank Michael Anania, poetry editor of Swallow Press during its early days in Chicago, and Peter Jay, editor of Anvil Press, for loyalty and support both early and late. Among poets who have offered criticism and encouragement at crucial stages during the twenty years covered by this book, I thank especially Igor Webb, Peter Michelson, Ernest Sandeen, Robert Hass, Richard Burns, and Göran Printz-Påhlson. For the pleasures of collaboration, and for permitting me to publish collaborative work in a book of my own, I thank Göran Printz-Påhlson and Vladeta Vucković. For his illustrations for the Swedish edition of *Batory & Lermontov*, and for his friendship and example, I thank Douglas Kinsey. For discussions touching particular problems of poetics which were far more important for me at various times than I initially realized, I thank my University of Notre Dame colleagues John Garvick, Sean Golden, Stephen Fredman and Joseph Buttigieg. I also want to thank the editors of journals which originally published the poems collected in *Bucyrus*, *Turns* and *Crossing*, particularly Charles Newman and Elliott Anderson of *TriQuarterly*, Daryl Hine of *Poetry* (Chicago), Michael Schmidt of *PN Review*, and Robert Boyers of *Salmagundi*. For first publishing the new poems in Section 6, grateful acknowledgement is made to Frederick Turner and *The Kenyon Review* ("To V.V.:

8

On Our Translation of the Kossovo Fragments"), to Andrew Motion and *The Poetry Review* ("Unpleasant Letter"), to Keith Tuma and *Chicago Review* ("Unpleasant Letter" and "E.P. in Crawfordsville"), to Hilary Davies and *Argo* ("Words for Karl Wallenda" and selections from "Northern Summer"), to Robert Boyers and *Salmagundi* (selections from "Northern Summer"), to Martin Booth and the Sceptre Press pamphlet series ("Rostropovich at Aldeburgh"), and to William Spanos and *Boundary 2* (the whole of "Northern Summer"). Several of the poems in this book have also been broadcast on the BBC *Poetry Now* program, and I wish to thank Fraser Steel for his interest and support.

I was born and grew up in Ohio, lived for three years in California, and then began living according to the pattern that has been constant since 1967: I teach for a living at the University of Notre Dame in South Bend, Indiana, but I write almost always in Britain: in London, Suffolk, Cambridge, and (recently) Fife. That I have been able to write where I feel both welcome and free, I owe to a number of grants and leaves from Notre Dame, to the hospitality of Clare Hall, Cambridge, and to the generosity of my wife's family, particularly that of her mother, Mrs Pamela Adams. *Crossing* was dedicated in part to Mrs Adams' house: Cherry Tree, Hacheston, Suffolk. For fifteen years it was a refuge for my family, but it is no longer ours, no longer hers. In his short essay "The Poet's Place" Donald Hall remarks that for those poets who respond to place "The poem wishes to attain—perhaps does attain, for a moment— a rare condition of blessedness, which the place sponsors." I can't speak for the success of poems responding to place in this book, but the wish of which Hall speaks was certainly there—and there can be no doubt at all about the sponsorship. Finally, I thank the lady whose name appears more often than any other in the poems that follow.

John Matthias
June, 1983

For Diana: A Ballad, A Book

I had in my charge two ladies
And I was the King of the West.
I had in my charge two ladies
And two of Angloria's best.

And the wind beat the rain at the window
And the wind beat the rain on the stair.
I bolted the doors and compartments.
I took down the ladies' bright hair.

And they set up a table, my beauties,
They filled it with wine and delights.
Fulfilled and complete were my duties;
Reward was an aeon of nights.

And the wind beat the rain at the window
And the wind beat the rain on the stair.
We ate and we drank and we drank and we ate
And we finished our banqueting there.

And I belched and arose from the table,
I swallowed a pickled red pear,
I hurried as fast as I'm able
To strip me a lady bare…

When suddenly face at the window,
Suddenly foot at the stair,
Suddenly sound of an army around
And a voice that split open the air.

It said: I'm the King of the West.
It said: You failed your quest.
Hand over your beauties
Go back to your duties
Get out and work with the rest.

Oh I was sent out in the wind and the rain
And I never set foot in that country again.

1
from *Bucyrus*

Triptych

He doesn't sleep. He sits.
He looks around.
Afraid of quiet, bits
Of dust and sound,
He doesn't sleep. He sits
And looks around.
He was in love, he thinks.
He cannot smile.
He reads his early poems
To learn his style.
He doesn't write. He was
In love. He thinks.
He scribbles at a pad
With colored inks.

II

There is no bed. One stands.
One walks about.
A fountain for the hands
Drips water out.
There is no pillow, sheet,
Or bed at all;
A fountain for the feet
Is in the hall.
A fountain for the feet
Or for the hands—
Oh, sit upon the floor!
A yellow needle
Pins a ballad to
The door.

III

The King was dead. Earth flat.
And women real.
Beside me Marcus sat.
We took our meal.
"I have his daughter, sir,
I have his bride.
A proper poem, my lord,
Will buy them tied.
A proper poem, my lord,
If you can write.
I'll have them in your bed
Tomorrow night."
And I remember that.
And I recall.
Beside me Marcus sat
And that was all.

Renaissance

The knocked-up look is back!
(old accurate Van Eyck):
the turned-up pointed shoes,
the twin-peaked cap.
Gentlemen, there's no one
here but Gentlemen.

And Ladies.

And the Court.

Virgins of St Denis
bare their privies for
the prince. And I am priest
and altar, consecrated host.
Bread and whiskey on
my loins, a wooden
phallus, nails:
I stiffen and endure.

Empty out the coffins, then.

Disinter the bones.

An Absence

Korok.

And of Korok, Kazi or Brelum
Teka or Tecta.

Libushka. Libushka
Of Korok, a sybil.

Weleska said: our lady
Libushka is dead.

But let us continue to rule.

The tithes were refused.
The clergymen were assaulted.
Henry IV deferred to
The Bishop of Bremen.

Excommunicate (about '97)
And damned, the men
Of that region deferred
To the women.

iii

"Hordes of devils are making for France!"
("The French, you know, are
A restless and turbulent people.")
Run the country in absence
Of Husband and Son?
Libushka of Korok, a sybil.

iv

A toad the size of a goose or a duck.
The rhetoric of crusades.

Five Lyrics from "Poem in Three Parts"

i

Sing-bonga, angered
by the smoke, sent
crows. Later he slept
in the furnace.

Sing-anga, earlier
and far away, a
fetus found and
burned:
>   "on that ash
>   erect a temple, Yakut shaman."

Yang & Yin
Yin & Yang

For the smith
and his bride,
these coals.

ii

could boil,
melt
  (ego in
    hand)
his world.

therefore feared
as agent
   ("public
   menace")

matter unre-
generate
mirrors
(crime).

Verbum dictum factum: god in
the vowels of the earth:

ascribe unto
these metals,
Hermes,
need.

          iii

(otherwise
perceive the imperfection
understand

not to imperfection
even otherwise
command

dross & refuse &
decay

ascend
condense)

Philosophy, he held, was out of hand.

          iv

Whether C. was
          duped "per doctrinam"
Whether C. knew
          Shuchirch at all

William de Brumley, "chaplain lately
dwelling with the Prior of Harmondsworth"—
does he lie?

Whether C. was a
victim or student...

        (hermaphroditic rebis
        there appeared.

        Probably not.)

        Probably not.

        later,
        after

   v

The still-providing
world is not
enough: we add.

Ponder matter
where impatient
sleepers wait.

And Aphrodite
saw her soul
was stone.

And Nargajuna
dreamed that
he was glad.

Between

Between here
and away
is a
way

and a point
to be made.

what matter
now
is how?

to leave is
to the point

it is

it is a way,

(and equally
the coffee
and the
calm.)

Diptych

Carpet flames.
Chain grip: incense
in a cup. Violins
and mandolins re-
corded. Oddly off.
Stumble dancer,
rafter slanting down.
(What is now beyond
you now my dear?)
Hold it (having
hardened) with a kiss.
He had lied
for years.

Zero on ice.
Tire spun: smoke
to three a.m. Hail
and also headlight
dimming. Oddly out.
Weep then weeper,
headlight out and hail.
(Who is now beside
me now and dear?)
Break it (having
buckled) with a fist.
She had cried
for years.

Arzeno Kirkpatrick

Should he, if the telephone rings,
pick it up? And if a knock should
come at the door? He ponders, Arzeno
Kirkpatrick, the questions. Another
occurs: what if a light should
suddenly flash in the yard?
It is late; Arzeno Kirkpatrick
is tired. He sips his tea and
smokes his cigarettes. He
ponders, Arzeno Kirkpatrick,
the questions.

There is a light in the yard.
The telephone rings.
There is an angry knocking at the door.

Swimming at Midnight

[*Near my grandparents' home at the outskirts of town, a stone quarry was established, then abandoned, nearly a hundred and fifty years ago. The early blasting hit water, and after many soundings were taken, the management concluded that they had uncovered a bottomless lake, fed, they surmised, by a sizeable underground river.*]

Under a pine and confusion:
ah! Tangles of clothes: (come
on, silly, nobody's here:) and
naked as fish, a boy and a girl.
(Nobody comes here: nobody looks:
nobody watches us watching us
watch.) Except the police.
Thighs slide into the moon.
Humbly, into the stars: Mirrored,
flashes a father's red eye, a
blue-bitten mother's red lip: No
Swimming Allowed In The Quarry
At Night. (Anyway, nevertheless
and moreover: feel how warm!) here,
among the reflections. (Feel the
water's mouth and its hands, feel
them imitate mine: can there truly
be any danger?) danger allowed in
the quarry at night? can people
really have drowned? (Now my body
is only water alive, and aeons
ago you were a fish growing
legs—) well, dust to dust, a
curious notion. But quarry water on
dust green with seed! Quarry water
forbidden on land after dark! What
young forms of vegetation emerge.
What new colors of light.

2
from *Turns*

For Diana

Look at these words.
What is there in them
You should tolerate
My absences, my silence.

As if they made a world
Where we could live, you
Offer me what I expect.

Should least. Last. And
Only look on circumspect.

Fathers

I never knew them.
Neither one. That
ancient Englishman
was deaf and in-
accessible—I

took his daughter
from his house.
He was dreaming
of ships, of Vienna,
his German assassin

sleeping under
his bed:
I never knew.
In Republican
Ohio, the man

I thought I
hated grew so
thin he'd slip
he said a wedding
ring around his

upper arm. Rheumatic,
he rode like a horse
his electrical in-
valid chair.
He was a judge

and should have
been a sailor...
Who'd stand no
nonsense, tell
them of the Empire

and by God Britannia,
chew his pipe
and try to
understand his girl—
twenty-one and

born when
he was fifty.
And if I'd known them,
either one, if I'm a
sailor now and should

have been a judge,
what son will talk
to me? What stranger
take my daughter from
a daughter's house?

Survivors

I

A letter arrives in answer
To mine—but six years late...
"John," it says,
                    "Dear John..." and
"I remember absolutely nothing.
What you say is probably
All true; for me those
Years are blank. I believe
You when you say you knew
Me then, that we were friends,
And yet I don't remember you
At all, or all those others
Who had names, or anyone. You see,

The fittest don't survive—
It's the survivors."

II

Like old women, burying their
Husbands, burying their sons, lasting
It out for years without their breasts
Or wombs, with ancient eyes,
Arthritic hands, and memories like
Gorgeous ships they launch
Despairingly to bring back all
Their dead, and which, as if constructed
By some clumsy sonneteer, betray them
Instantly and sink without a trace.

III

Or women not so old—
                    but always
Women, not the men who knock
Their brains and bodies against
Fatal obstacles & spit their blood
On pillows & their hearts on sleeves
At forty-five to die of being fit.

I've known a woman keep her watch
Beside a bed of botched ambition
Where her man lay down & took
Five years to die...

And though I drove one January night
Through freezing rain into Ohio—
And though I hurried,
Seeking the words of the dying—
All I found was a turning circle of women,
All I heard was the lamentation of survivors.

Part of an Answer

The man who forced the
window with a wrench
was never there, I
opened it myself: you
suffered anyway your

mugging and his lust.
If we really pulled
our knives in bed
and slashed, you'd
never ask. I'd never

say: responsibility
ends. Your piety!
I'll live on water
and dried peas.
Poems, love, poems!

I try to make the
evil things, secondary
worlds, though even
a Magus said it—primary
there—no world

but the world. And
the Word? A girl
who died for poetry
once wrote: to crawl
between the lines

of print and sleep. She
wanted that. Accretion
then, and possibility.
You wind your watch
and I attend.

If Not a Technical Song American: Statement, Harangue, and Narrative

I STATEMENT

Just last night I read your poems to the President.
You don't believe me, but I really did.
He broke down completely and
Wept all over his desk.
Now that I've done my work, you can relax.
Everything's going to be o.k.

And I read your poems to a joint session of Congress.
I read your poems to the FBI and the CIA.
Now that I've done my work, you can relax.
Everything's going to be o.k.

II HARANGUE

Your tired evasions, euphemism-lies.
Civilized man and his word-hoard.
Will you be relinquant
Or relinquished.

Name and Title. Religion and Rank.
Put a check in the column.
Put a check in the bank.

If you'd be only a little bit clever.
If you'd be occasionally.
If you'd be forever.

If you'd be my government.
If you'd be my gal.
If you'd be my treason and my tongue.

If anything articulate remains,
Identify the numbers by the names.

III   Narrative

Cachectic, cachectic.
Heart rate grossly irregular.
Jugular venous distention.
Systolic expansile pulse.

Right ventricular lift.
Left ventricular tap.
Murmur along the sternal borders.
Pulmonary edema.

All piezometers installed
In the boreholes.
Static and dynamic
Cone penetration made.

Infra-red results
Allow mathematical models.
I hope I was never
Complacent: Seismology.

BUT IF I WAS IN LOVE WITH YOU?
I was in love with you, I think.
I think I didn't have the heart.

No, I never even thought to move the earth.

For John, After His Visit: Suffolk, Fall

Soldati's band shook Patty Fenelon's house
    last Spring so badly that the
Bookcase toppled down and spilled the cheap
    red wine on three authentic South
Bend, Indiana drunks....
                    For you, who love
    the elegiac and, if you believed
The arts you practice had in fact a chance
    of life at all, would prophesy
A new Romantic muse for all of us, how
    can I speak generously enough
About the life we've shared—the rich neurotic
    squalor of the midwest's Catholic
Mecca (...you a convert, me a Roman guest—
    cloistered there together preaching
Culture to the grandsons of Italian immigrants,
    the sons of Irishmen and Poles)?

You must, you always told me,
    have intensity. Half your students
Always thought you mad. Like Gordon
    Liddy on a job you'd go
To them bewigged and bearded bearing with
    you some incongruous foreign
Object—a Henry James harpoon or a Melvillian
    top hat—while through the hidden
Speakers blared your tape of Colin Davis and
    the BBC crooning Elgar on the
Last night of the Proms. Light in darkness, John!
    And all your manic gestures were serene.

Yeats to Lady Gregory, Nineteen Hundred & Four:
    "I did not succeed at Notre Dame."
He began to think his notions seemed "the thunder
    of a battle in some other star"; the thought
Confused him and he lectured badly; later he
    told tales with the "merry priests".

So you were not the first to feel estranged! And
　　　oh the thunder of your battle in that
Other star, its foolishness and grace. Beyond that
　　　fiddle, though, intensity was real
Enough for both of us.

How was I to know, returning from the dusty
　　　attic room where I had gone, where
I had often gone from midnight until three, and
　　　seeing you stare vacantly across
Your desk and through your lighted study
　　　window at the February snow that
You should truly be in love with my young
　　　friend, with that same lonely girl?

Was that the week you thought your son was ill?
　　　When you waited frightened while the
Severed head of Johnny's siamese cat melted grinning
　　　in its package of dry ice padlocked in
The Greyhound baggage room in Indianapolis? The
　　　tests were negative, the bites
And scratches healed....
　　　　　　　　　　　Hiking on a treadmill
　　　at the clinic, I tested badly on a
Winter afternoon myself. I traded polysyllables
　　　with cardiologists who hooked me to their
Apparatus, checked my pressures, watched my blips
　　　on television screens, and asked me all
The secrets of my heart....

Once we hiked together on the muddy banks of the
　　　St Joseph, then across a farm. Your
Children ran ahead. They led you, while you
　　　talked in words they could not hear,
Haranguing me about the words you sometimes spoke
　　　when you would only speak, to credit
For a moment, because they looked at all around
　　　them, tree and bush and flower, because
They did not name and did not need to name, the
　　　eluctable modality of all you saw.

38

What more homely elegiacs, John, than this:
    reading backwards in a diary from
May—May to January, January twenty-fifth... and
    all my pulses skip. My father's gestures
Of exhausted resignation cease; he drops his cup
    of ovaltine and stares into my
Mother's eyes amazed.... No dream, even, did he
    send me in my mourning time, no news
At all.... As a child I saw irregularities signaled
    in the pulsings of distended veins
Running up his temples and across his wrists:
    more affaires de cœur....
                                    You made
Your trip among the dead ten years ago
    but found a Christian God along
The way in Barcelona. Did I take for politics
    your strange Falangist quips
The day we met?

December last, a month before my father's death,
    a quiet Christmas eve with sentimental
And nostalgic talk, some carolling.... Suddenly
    the blood. Stalking through a dark
And quiet house with automatic rifle and grenades
    you'd kick a bedroom door to bits and
Blast the sleeping couple in their bed, sprinkling
    holy water everywhere—your own obsessive
Dream. "I must have savagery", a wealthy British
    poet told me, leaving for the States.
I've gone the other way. My next door neighbor
    pounded at my door on Christmas eve; his
Bleeding wounds were real. What was all of England
    to a single one of his desires? When
I needed help you harbored me.

I wonder if our quarrel touches writing desks,
    like Mandelstam's with Pasternak. The
Greater man required none, the other poet did.
    Behind each artifact of any worth,

Cocteau insists, there is a house, a lamp, a fire,
 a plate of soup, a rack of pipes,
And wine. The bourgeoisie as bedrock. Mandelstam
 would crouch in corners listening to
The burning in his brain. If you're a Russian
 Jew because I am a wanton I am Catholic.

So what's the Devil's wage? Your riddling military
 metaphors unwind from Clausewitz and you
Will not say; your Faust, de Sade in neat quotations
 will not do. In London monographs on
Mahler are delivered in the morning post intended
 for the eyes of diplomats on holiday in
Devon—the still & deadly music of the IRA. One
 by one these books explode… In the hands
Of an unlucky clerk, the lap of an astonished secretary
 dreaming of her lover.

Stranger, then, and brother! John, these last three
 nights I've listened for you here,
Listened for you here where off the North Sea
 early Autumn winds bring down the
Twigs and bang the shutters of this house
 you came to bringing with you
Secrets and your difficult soul. In disintegrating
 space we are an architecture of sounds.
And you are not returning.

Once for English Music

i

This, this is marvelous,
    this is simply too good—
I am their song, Jeremiah!
    Elgar on The Folk.

And I have worked for forty years
    and Providence denies
Me hearing of my work. So I submit:
    God is against it,

Against art. And I have worked
    for forty years and
Providence denies. And Strauss (R.),
    1905: I drink

To the welfare of the first
    English progressive.
And Gerontius: pray for me, my friends,
    who have no strength to pray.

ii

And who would not put out—with his mother
Or his Queen—the night light,

Toothbrush, bathrobe and condom,
Run the bath, switch on the stereo,

Plug in the fire, and wait for time
To reverse, wait for a Prince to rise

From the dead & conduct his affairs?
Neither you nor I, neither mine nor yours.

iii

There in the James Gunn portrait,
There, almost, in the Beecham life—

Delius who wasn't really English,
Delius who got around:

Dying, did he summon in his cripple's dream
A syphilitic and promiscuous librettist

(In a summer garden, or on hearing the
First cuckoo in Spring)?

He would compose.
He would have his way with words.

iv

During the performance
   of an overture, said Shaw,
By one of the minor Bachs,
   I was annoyed
By what I took to be the jingling
   of a bell-wire somewhere.
But it was Dr Parry. Playing the
   cembalo part... on a
Decrepit harpsichord.

v

Fluctuating sevenths,
　　fluctuating thirds.
I'll play it on my flute
　　the way it sounds.

In Surrey, in Sussex,
　　airs against the harmon-
Izing organist from
　　Worthing....

For Why Do The Roses?
　　Because we sing enchanted.
Because we chant
　　And sing.

Three Around a Revolution

I   A Gift

He is the Tribune of The People,
He is Babeuf. The others speculate,

But he is Babeuf. The others
Speculate and steal. Gracchus

Out of Plutarch, he takes
The crudely fashioned knife

Made by his son from a candlestick
For his (the father's) suicide.

He hones it on his eloquent tongue.
He says, smiling enigmatically:

Here, it is yours. Do what you can.

II   Alternatives

One announces in papers:
Seeking the patronage of the rich

To further my work. For a decade
It will always be noon.

Nobody's wealth intervenes
Between freedom and time.

One in despair discharges a gun:
Nevertheless, he goes on writing

Noblesse oblige with seven balls
Of shot in his brain.

Making accurate measurements,
Another says: Here we may build,

Here we may bathe, here we may breathe.

III A LETTER

There must be horses, there must be women,
There must be lawsuits. There must, moreover

And eventually, be justice. There must be words.
I write down words. Are we lost in our names?

Yesterday I spoke for hours and nobody stirred.
Rapt. They cheered. I am a hero.

I said words like *action, money, love, rights*
And was moved to elegance, alliteration,

Saying, apropos of what I did not know,
Palfrey, palindrome, pailing, palinode, palisade.

Bakunin in Italy

Wagner's face is still illuminated
Over Dresden in that fire I fed

And in the glow of it I see my sister
Walking through the snow beside Turgenev.

Did I spit my teeth out in the Peter-Paul
Only to release the homicidal genius

Of Nachaev? I should have been a Jesuit,
A Mason. Castrati sing the Internationale

And dance the choreography of Karl Marx.
I should have been a tenor playing

Sophie Hatzfeldt in an *opéra bouffe*
By Ferdinand Lassalle.

Alexander Kerensky at Stanford

He rose one Winter from his books
To sit among the young, unrecognized.

It was 1963. It was 1917.
He sipped his coffee & was quite anonymous.

Students sat around him at their union
Talking politics: Berkeley, Mississippi.

A sun-tanned blonde whose wealthy father
Gave her all his looks and half his money

Whispered to her sun-tanned lover:
"Where *is* Viet Nam?"

He thought no thought of theirs.
In his carrel at the Hoover Institute

He had the urns of all his ancient enemies.
Their dust was splattered on his purple tie.

Six for Michael Anania

I   TRITHEMIUS

Orifiel reigned:
    March 15
        the first year of the world.

So, Trithemius, timid and wise.
So, Agrippa. Light!

Paid the debts at Sponheim.
Drove the lazy monks.
God's breath, good books: stone.

Vulgar speak of vulgar things.
So, Agrippa. Light!

Maximilian in my
    cunning circle
        trod.

II   AGRIPPA VON NETTESHEIM

Nothing less than total reform
Mystical. Of the world.

Margaret of Austria, O Mirific Maid,

August, divine, and very clement chick,
I'm on the dole.

The Nobility of Women Folk—
Exalt I phrases here…
Dollars for the scholars, sweetheart; smile.

So that Franciscan calls me heretic.
So Inquisitor Savini burns his share.

Frogs' eyes. Mule piss.
Everyone's Pythagorean here.

III   PARACELSUS

All things change save one.
All things one save change.

Re-ligare means unite again.

Areopagite of Athens,
Follow *now*. Where?

The patients of the Galenians died.

And in her hand
   (the Queen's)
      I'll put a rose.
And in his hand
   (the King's)
      I'll put a golden crown.

And in the sea aboard their ship
The King he'll take his Queen.

The patients of the Galenians died.

IV   NOSTRADAMUS

The curious words remain. The seer sees.
Single combat on a lawn; the bloody axe.

Out of time, he travels in it still.
Catherine de Medici knows. Henry II is warned.

The act occurs as it is seen the act occurred.

Out of time, he traveled in it still.
Catherine de Medici knew. Henry II was warned.

The curious words remained. The seer saw.
Single combat on a lawn; the bloody axe.

The act occurred as it is seen the act occurs.

V ROSENCREUTZ TO SAINT-GERMAIN

We did not mean Brother Martin.
We did not mean 30 Years War.

We did not mean Huguenots
Or St Bartholomew's Eve.

We did not mean property.
We did not mean money.

We did not mean Pope
Or the Place de la Grève.

But no more maneuvers.
All are vowed to death.

Too late. I have done all I can.

VI

Qualities tend
To Perfection.

We may assist.

Double Sonnet on the Absence of Text: "Symphony Matis der Maler", Berlin, 1934:—Metamorphoses

I

The eschatology of Jews and Christian heretics:
Unearthly metal glows. *Schafft er nicht mehr*—
He lies among his tools.
Geh hin und bilde. Geh hin und bilde
Polyptich as polyphony. Medieval modes,
Matis: Gothardt, Neithardt. Grunewald
To historians, *der Maler.*
Father of no child though, Regina; father
Of his altarpiece at Isenheim, father
Of his torments, his tormentors,
Dying in obscurity at Halle building mills.
Geh hin und bilde. For Albricht, Luther
Or for Muntzer? *Geh hin und bilde.*
The pointing finger of an evangelic hand
Outlasts apocalypse.

II

The libretto: that's the crux, the words.
Because of that the senile Strauss would
Play *Gebrauchsmusik* for Goebbels who, while
Furtwängler's applauded by the partisans
Of Brecht or Grosz or Benn, sits
On hams beside the corpse of Wagner.
Oh that Hindemith should feel the pull
Of Matis: What's the distance, then, from
Buchenwald to Yale? *Ist, dass du
Schaffst und bildest, genug?*
Abandoned, all the words: for what
They cannot settle will be left alone.
Leaving us just where, Professor?
Contemplating cosmogonic harmonies with Kepler.
In oblivion with courage and acoustics.

Turns: Toward a Provisional Aesthetic and a Discipline

I

The scolemayster levande was the toun
and sary of hit semed everuch one.
The smal quyt cart that covert was and hors...
to ferien his godes. To ferien his godes
quere he was boun.

The onelych thyng of combraunce (combraunce)
was the symphonye
(saf a pakke of bokes)
that he hade boghte the yere
quen he bithoght
that he wolde lerne to play.

But the zele woned (zele woned).
He neuer couthe ani scylle.

II

And so the equivalent
              (the satisfactory text.
squ'elles sont belles
              sont pas fidèles. rough
west-midland, hwilum andgit
of andgiete: the rest is not
              a word for word defense....

III

And make him known to 14th-century men
Even when everything favors the living?
Even if we could reverse that here
I know you've read and traveled too.

52

So Destination or Destiny: *Quere He Was Boun!*
And yet to introduce the antecedent place.
Restrictive clause; sense of the referent noun.
A tilted cart is a cart with an awning.

> Langland has it "keured"
> John of Mandeville "coured"
> Wycliffe "keuered"

> But "covert" in Arimathaea

Personal luggage: not the same as merchandise.
Cursor Mundi's "gudes"; Purity's "godes"

This is personal luggage / destination / travel

> Harp and pipe and symphonye

> (saf a pakke of bokes)

IV

Where dwelle ye if it tell to be?

> at the edge
>   of the toun?
> at the edge
>   of the toun?

Levande was.
He Levande Was The Toun.

Reason the nature of place
Reason he can praise
Reason what the good-doing doctor said

> Rx.:cart   (that covert was & hors)

Dull ache in the hip is probably gout.
Painful nodes of calcium—(neck & in the ears).
Palpitations, flutters. Stones in the gland.

    food to avoid?   drink

       (put him in the cart)

    Rx.:bibliography
    Rx.:map

    V

The metaphysicality of Hermetic thought—
Let him think o' that! (Problem is he
Still enjoys cunt...)

... instrument was ay thereafter
Al his own combraunce...

Sary of hit semed everuch one.

Torn between disgust & hope
He simply never couthe...

antiquorum aegyptiorum
oh, ... imitatus...

    VI

All day long it rains. He travels
All day long. Wiping water from
His eyes: and twenty miles? and
Twenty miles? Fydlers nod & smile.

Cycles pass him. Cars pass him.
Buses full of tourists...

Dauncers & Minstrels, Drunkards
And Theeves. Whooremaisters,
Tossepottes; Maskers, Fencers
And Rogues; Cutpurses, Blasphemers
Counterfaite Egyptions...

Greek, Arabic, Medieval Latin,
Mis-translated, misconceived.
More than just for his disport

      who loveth daliaunce

who falleth   (o who falleth)

far behinde...

    VII

That supernatural science,
That rare art should seem...

      here among
      a randy
      black-billed

      ilk

Les traductions sont comme les femmes. And time to get off of her
toes. Idiomatic: toes. Lorsqu'elles sont belles. I should apologize,
then: to apologize. The schoolmaster was leaving the village, and
everybody seemed sorry. Simple as that. The miller lent him the
cart and horse to carry his goods. Simple as that. And no particular
trouble with the words. Scolemayster: 1225 in the *Life of St
Katherine*. But you change the spelling, see, to conform with the
dialect. Levande was: *The Destruction of Troy*, "all the Troiens
lefton". But use the participial construction. Sary of hit: see the
Lay Folks Mass Book. The city of his destination. Twenty miles off.
Quite sufficient size for his effects. The only cumbersome article

(save the pack of books) was: count on the medieval mind to be sympathetic. Though I come after hym with hawebake/I speke in prose and lat hym rymes make. My general principles I take from the King (and his Queen). Tha boc wendan on Englisc. Hwilum word be word. Hwilum andgit of andgiete. Swa swa ic hie geliornode. It would be idle and boring to rehearse. Here what is available. Let me simply indicate the manner. Take sulphur from Sol for the fire and with it roast Luna. From which will the word issue forth... *If* the given appeared in a verifiable text. *If* the given was truly equivalent.

The usual procedures are the following: (1) To ignore altogether: "make no effort to explain the fundamentals". (2) To drop apologetic footnotes: "I'm sorry, but I simply cannot understand this esoteric sort of thing". (3) To make suggestive remarks while hurrying on to something else: "*If* the given appeared in a verifiable text. *If* the given was truly equivalent". But the schoolmaster was leaving the village, and everybody seemed sorry. *Jude the Obscure,* paragraph one, a neat linguistic exercise. Written by Thomas Hardy in 1895. And such a revelation makes the art available to the vulgar. Who will abuse and discredit? *Keeper of secret wisdom, agent of revelation, vision, and desire:* THIS IS THE QUESTION WE MUST ALWAYS RAISE.

Now some of the obscure, like some of the lucid, do not become proletarianized. Unlike the majority of their kind, they are not cast down from the ruling class to produce a commodity which both enslaves them and enslaves the exploited labourers with whom they are objectively allied. Perhaps they hold teaching jobs in public schools or universities; perhaps they have an inherited income. In any case, some maintain their Hermetic privilege. They are not obliged to live by their art or to produce for the open market. Such unproletarianized obscure are revolted by the demands of a commercialized market, by the vulgarity of the mass-produced commodity supplied to meet it. And revulsion ultimately tells (1) on their sex life (2) on their health.

While a relationship of cause and effect is established between obscure and lucid organizations emerging from the division of labour and the consequent dialectical evolution of social reality, such becomes, we know, increasingly separated from the actual productive function of society, from sleep. This gives us pause. "The point is that the notion of invariancy inherent by definition to the concept of the series, if applied to all parameters, leads to a uniformity of configurations that eliminates the last traces of unpredictability, of surprise." This gives us pause.

And so the system and its adherents are the villains; license, conspiracy, and nihilism are the virtues of the heroes: or: The system itself becomes a context for heroics; license, conspiracy, and nihilism become the crimes of the villains; acceptance of convention and austere self-discipline become the virtues of the heroes. The schoolmaster is forever an intermediary: the shape of his life is determined by the nature of society: the nature of his art seeks to determine the shape of society by administering to its nature. And intermediacy ultimately tells (1) on his sex life (2) on his health.

But make him known to 14th-century men even when everything favors the living. Reason the nature of place. Reason he can praise. Reason that he travels in a cart. With Cursor Mundi's "gudes"; with Purity's "godes". With Joseph of Arimathaea, turns: to elliptically gloss.

Double Derivation, Association, and Cliché: from *The Great Tournament Roll of Westminster*

I

The heralds wear their tabards correctly.
Each, in his left hand, carries a wand.
Before and after the Master of Armour
Enter his men: three of them carry the staves.
The mace bearer wears a yellow robe.
In right & goodly devysis of apparyl
The gentlemen ride.
The double-curving trumpets shine.

Who breaks a spear is worth the prize.

II

Or makes a forest in the halls of Blackfriars
at Ludgate whych is garneychyd wyth trees & bowes,
wyth bestes and byrds; wyth a mayden
syttyng by a kastell makyng garlonds there;
wyth men in woodwoos dress,
wyth men of armes....
                    Or Richard Gibson
                        busy
with artificers and labour, portages and ships:
busy with his sums and his accounts:
for what is wrought by carpenters & joyners,
karrovers & smiths...
(Who breaks a spear is worth the prize)
Who breaks a schylld on shields
a saylle on sails
a sclev upon his lady's sleeves;

who can do skilfully the spleter werke,
whose spyndylles turn

Power out of parsimony, feasting
Out of famine, revels out of revelation:—
Out of slaughter, ceremony.
When the mist lifts over Bosworth.
When the mist settles on Flodden.

Who breaks a spear is worth the prize.

III

The double-curving trumpets shine:
   & cloth of gold.
The challengers pass...

Well, & the advice of Harry Seven:—
(or the Empress Wu, depending
where you are):
We'll put on elegance later.
We'll put off art.
No life of Harry the Seven
   there in the works of the Bard...
(No Li Po on Wu)
An uninteresting man? Parsimonious.

Wolsey travels in style...
        & on the Field of Cloth of Gold
   & in the halls at Ludgate
a little style....
Something neo-Burgundian
(Holy, Roman, & bankrupt) illuminating
Burgkmairs in *Der Weisskunig* & *Freydal.*
Rival Maximilian's mummeries, his
dances and his masques, his
armouries & armourers the mark.

Hammermen to King, his prize; King
to hammermen: guard, for love of progeny,
the private parts!

     (My prick's bigger
than *your* prick, or Maxi's prick,
or James')

   IV

     & like the Burgkmairs
these illuminations:—
where, o years ago, say twenty-two or
say about five hundred,
cousins in the summertime would
ritualize their rivalries
in sumptuous tableaux.
Someone holds a camera. Snap.
In proper costume, Homo Ludens wears
Imagination on his sleeve.

But chronicle & contour fashion
out of Flodden nothing but the truth.
The deaths, in order & with dignity,
of every child: I remember that.

Who breaks a spear is worth the prize.

   V

Who breaks a schylld on shields
  a saylle on sails
a sclev upon his lady's sleeves...
And in the north, & for the nearer rival.
Who meteth Coronall to Coronall, who beareth
a man down:—down the distance to Westminster,
down the distance in time.

For the pupil of Erasmus,
for the rival of the Eighth,
a suitcase dated Flodden full of relics.
Shipped Air France, they're scattered
at the battle of the Somme.
It intervened, the news:
it intervenes

As, at the Bankside, Henry makes
a masque at Wolsey's house and, certain
cannons being fired, the paper
wherewith one of them is stopped
does light the thatch, where being
thought at first but idle smoke,
it kindles inwardly consuming
in the end
the house
the Globe

> The first & happiest hearers of the town
> among them, one Sir Henry Wotton

Largely Fletcher's work

VI

O, largely spleter werke
that certain letters could be sent
unto the high & noble excellent Princess
the Queen of England from her dear & best beloved
Cousin Noble Cueur Loyall with knowledge of
the good and gracious fortune of the birth
of a young prince:
> & to accomplish certain
feats of arms the king (signed Henry R)
does send four knights...

> & sends to work his servant Richard Gibson
> on the Revels and Accounts

& sends the children in the summertime to play
& sends the rival Scott a fatal surrogate
from Bosworth, makes an end
to *his* magnificence.

Slaughter out of ceremony, famine
out of feasting, out of power
parsimony, out of revels
revelation...

    As an axe in the spine can reveal,
   as an arrow in the eye.

Who breaks a spear is worth the prize.

  VII

And what is wrought by carpenters & joyners,
by karrovers & smiths, is worth the prize;
and what is wrought by labour.
For those who play. Of alldyr pooles & paper,
whyght leed and gleew, yern hoopes of sundry
sortes; kord & roopes & naylles:—
All garneychyd at Ludgate. With
trees & bows. All garneychyd with
cloth of Gold.

    The challengers pass

And deck themselves outrageously
in capes & plumes and armour...
And out to play: making in the summertime
a world against all odds, and with
its Winter dangers.

    In a garden, old men play at chess.
    In the Summer. In the Winter, still.

Who will decorate the golden tree,
Employ properly the captive giant
And the dwarf? Who will plead
His rights despite decrepitude...?

        I reach for words as in a photograph
       I reach for costumes in a trunk:

An ancient trunk (an ancient book)

        a saylle, a schylld, a sclev

     a yellow robe, a wand—

        pipes & harpes & rebecs,
        lutes & viols for a masque.

Where double-curving trumpets shine
The challengers pass.

Who breaks a spear is worth the prize.

Clarifications for Robert Jacoby

("Double Derivation...", Part IV, ll. 1-10; Part VII, ll. 1-15, 22-28)

A moment ago, Robert, I thought I was watching
    a wren, the one which nests
By my window here, fly, dipping & rising,
    across this field in Suffolk
So like the one we used to play in, in Ohio,
    when we were boys. But it was
Really something that you, Dr Jacoby, would
    be able to explain by pointing out
To me in some expensive, ophthalmological text
    the proper Latin words.

It was no wren (still less the mythological bird
    I might have tried to make it)—
But just defective vision: one of those spots
    or floating motes before the eyes
That send one finally to a specialist. Not
    a feathered or a golden bird,
Nothing coming toward me in the early evening
    mist, just a flaw, as they say,
In the eye of the beholder.

Like? in a way?
    the flaw in the printer's eye
(the typesetter's, the proof-
    reader's) that produced and then
Let stand that famous line
    in Thomas Nashe's poem about the plague,
"Brightness falls from the air",
    when what he wrote was, thinking
Of old age and death, "Brightness
    falls from the *hair*".

I wonder if you remember all those games
    we used to play: the costumes,

All the sticks & staves, the whole complicated
    paraphernalia accumulated to suggest
Authentic weaponry and precise historical dates,
    not to mention exact geographical places,
All through August and September—the months you
    visited. You wanted then, you said,
To be an actor, and your father—a very practical
    lawyer—said he found that funny, though
I think we both intuited
    that he was secretly alarmed.

With little cause. You were destined—how obvious
    it should have been!—to be professional,
Respectable, and eminent. Still, you put in time
    and played your child's part
With skill and grace.

There is a photograph of us taken, I believe,
    in 1950. Your plumed hat (a little
Tight) sits sprightly on your head, your cape
    (cut from someone's bathrobe) hangs
Absurdly down your back, and in your hand you
    brandish the sword of the patriarch
Himself, grandfather M., Commander in Chief
    Of the United Spanish War Vets.
                            My
Plumed hat is slightly better fitting, if less
    elegant, my sword a fencing foil with
A rubber tip, my cape the prize: something from
    the almost legitimate theatre, from
My father's role in a Masonic play where he spoke,
    once each year before initiations
On some secret, adult stage, lines he practiced
    in the kitchen all the week before:
Let the jewelled box of records be opened
    and the plans for the wall by the
South west gate be examined!

The photographer, it seems, has irritated us.
    We scowl. The poses are not natural.

Someone has said Simon says stand here, look
    there, dress right, flank left;
Someone, for the record, intervenes. Or has
    James arrived? Our cousin from the
East side of Columbus who, with bicycles
    and paper routes and baseballs
Wanted you in time as badly then as I could
    want you out of it. A miniature
Adult, he looked askance at our elaborate
    rituals. He laughed outright,
Derisively. No mere chronicler, he was reality
    itself. I hated him.

Of whom I would remind myself when asking you:
    do you remember? a world of imagination,
Lovely and legitimate, uncovering, summer after
    summer, a place that we no longer go,
A field we do not enter now, a world one tries
    to speak of, one way or another,
In a poem. Robert! Had the jewelled box
    of records been opened and the plans
For the wall by the south west gate been examined,
    news: that he, not you and I, made
Without our knowledge, without our wigs and
    epaulets, with bricks he had a right
To throw, binding rules for our splendid games.

How remote it all must seem to you who joined
    him with such dispatch. One day, I
Suppose, I'll come to you in California saying
    to you frankly: cure me if you can.
Or to some other practicing your arts. Until then,
    what is there to talk about except
This book of photographs? And what they might
    have made of us, all those aunts,
Clucking at our heels, waddling onto Bosworth field
    or Flodden with their cameras. And why
They should have come, so ordinary and so mortal,
    to bring back images like this one

Turning yellow in a yellow book. Brightness fell
        from the hair

Of whom I would be worthy now, of whom I think
        about again as just outside my window
A child plays with a stick. And jumps on both feet
        imitating, since she sees it in the field
(With a stick in its beak), a wren. She enters
        the poem as she enters the field. I will
Not see her again. She goes to her world of stick
        and field and wren; I go to my world
Of poem. She does not know it, and yet she is here:
        here in the poem as surely as there
In the field, in the dull evening light, in the world
        of her imagining, where, as the mist descends,
She is a wren.

As I write that down she is leaving the field.
        She goes to her house where her
Father and mother argue incessantly, where
        her brother is sick. In the house
They are phoning a doctor. In the poem—
        because I say so,
                        because I say once more
That she enters the world of her imagining
        where, as the mist descends,
She is a wren—
        She remains in the field.

East Anglian Poem

I

Materials of Bronze and of Iron—

    linch-pins and chariot wheels, nave-bands
and terret-rings: harness mounts, fittings, and
bridle-bits: also a sword, an axe: also a
golden torc
                    But the soils
                    are acid here

                    and it rains

Often there's only the mark of a tool on a bone
Often there's nothing at all

II

They herded oxen and sheep   They hunted the deer
They made a simple pottery, spun yarn   They scratched
in the earth to little effect
                    They were afraid

        of him

      here, with his armour

           thigh and skull unearthed
              beside the jawbone of his horse

Afraid of him who
      feared these others, Belgae,
speaking Celtic too, but building oppida, advancing,
turning sod with coulters and with broad-bladed ploughs.

(Caesar thought them civilized—
                    which meant familiar

They minted coins

They made war on a sophisticated scale)

III

Sub Pellibus:

        Rectangular tents in orderly lines
        and round the camp a ditch.
        Palisade stakes. Rows of javelins
        with soft iron shanks, the semi-
            cylindrical shields.

                    Second Augusta here—
            with auxilia: archers and slingers,
                            mercenary Gauls.

He saw them on parade:

        their elegant horses, their leathers
        studded with gilt, their silvered pendants and
        the black niello inlay of their fittings
                and their rings

        their helmets made an apparition
        of the face: apertures for eyes. Their
        jerkins were embroidered, their yellow plumes and
                scarlet banners sailed in the wind.

        So they'd propitiate their gods.

He saw them on parade:

        to his north and east
        the boundary was the sea

iron pikes were driven
in the Waveney and Yare
   to his west the fenlands
forest to the south
   and south as well
between the trees and fens
   at Wandlebury here
along a narrow belt of chalk
   no more than eight
miles wide

                    his ramparts rose

                    (where certain grave-goods lie)

   IV

Within his hornworks
Behind his stone and timber walls
Below his towers and beneath his ample crop

      these early dead

                    (he saw the Trinovantes destroyed
                    who later saw Caratacus in chains)

      Their armlets and their
      toe-rings still adorn. Bronze
      bowls, amphorae, still provide.

         … and magic tokens there
      and writings there corrupted.
      With all their stolen coins,
      a carnyx there to play.

And stood up in the marshes many days.
Nor cried for meat.
Nor longed for any cup.

Consider what they were before
that men could suffer labour.

And feed upon the roots and barks of trees.

V

Before him and unknown to him and
southward came the stones: dolerite-blue
with tiny bits of felspar. From the Mt Prescelly
outcrops—Carn Meini, Foel Trigarn

      "Lord, and you must climb the holy peak"

Before him and unknown to him
  the first charioteers
    Before him, the first tamer of horses.

        He saw the hare run
        toward the sun, the

        mistletoe and sickle
        in the tree

        From the woods and the bogs
        they began to assemble

After the flat-bottom boats in the shallows of Mona

VI

After the incantations and the libations
After the auguries in the grove of the dishonored queen
After the spectral bride at the mouth of the Thames

     Did the tethered swans fly above him?
     Did the deer follow behind?

And after the pounding of magic into the swords?

From the confiscated lands
From the Calendar of Rites
From the Forward Policy of Rome

From the open hands of
     frightened and obsequious client-kings
From the pride of the Legatus
From the procurator's greed

     From the Divine House of Tiberius Claudius
       His octastyle temple and His Name
     NUMEN AUGUSTI
       From the hands of the Goddess of Death

The tethered swans flew above him
And the deer followed behind

Epilogue from a New Home

for Toby Barkan

There's a plague pit
    just to the edge of the village.
Above it, now mostly covered with grass,
    a runway for B-17s: (American
Pilots back from industrial targets). Tribes
    gathered under my window;
They'd sack an imperial town: I'll wave
    to my wife at the end of the Roman road.

At night I said
    (the odd smell of the house recalling home)
"My father sits up in his grave.
    I'm too unstrung to love you now. Look:
Children play in the garden with bones."

Enclosed within a boundary of stones
    they died in isolation. All of us have
Colds; we visit the parish church and read: "Names.
    The numbers of persons who died of bubonic plague."
Grey-stone cottages across the road,
    a stream at the end of the church-yard,
Giant harvesters working the mechanized farms....

Yesterday I walked to see the black,
    malignant huts that held the bombs.
After the war, nobody tore them down. Some
    are full of hay. Mechanics counted, standing
There, the number of planes that returned. I don't
    understand the work men did in the fields, or do.
I don't know the names of the crops. I don't
    know the uses of gears.
A church has grown on every hill like a tree.

Green on green: texture, shade, & shadows:
    opening out, folding in, surrounding.

Before the planes, someone counted ships: counted
        once that ancient one across the Deben
Where, from Woodbridge, you can almost see the site
        where his retainers set about to bury it,
A cenotaph, a King's.

Cynouai says: "I don't like my name. I won't have
        a name and I'll just be a girl."
Laura, three and deferential, understands. I open
        a bottle of wine.

A whir of looms where wool was wealth:
        (*nidings voerk, nidings voerk*) the baths long
Drained, the polyglot army long before withdrawn.
        If the Trinovantian coins & the legionary oaths,
If the pentatonic lyre in the Royal Ship
        prefigure here a merchant—*upon his head*
A *Flaundrish bever hat*—,
                                is that more odd
        than that my children's rhyme recalls
The plague, the unattended fields & the dissipation
        of the feudal claims, or that the final
Metamorphosis of Anna's luck should find its
        imagery—like Christ's—in bas-reliefs
Depicting animals domesticated by domesticating
        Saxon heirs?

We picnic by these graves, these strata of
        the dead: Celtic, Roman, Viking, English—
All of them killers, all of them dead, they'd moralize
        on one another's end. Christian to pagan, power
To power, and I am also implicated here: the woodwose
        in the spandrels of a door lifts up his club,
A voice begins to speak of Fifteen Signs....

Ah, Toby Barkan,
        this is not the poem you asked me for.
Waiting for the Wickham Market train a year ago I
        sat near Liverpool Street and wrote down notes:

About your early marriage and the joy of it,
    about the way it lasted—all that joy:
About a painting left unfinished for a year,
    a painter saying that he wanted more
From life than art—
    more than just to be competent:
Meaning that he wanted you instead,
    and his son, my oldest friend,
and his son's wife,
    and his son's son and his daughter....

And meaning, I suppose,
    that competence is dangerous and deceptive,
Meaning that he'd quit:
    before he tricked himself, before he'd
Grown so old he'd suffer for it all.

And I wrote down notes about his
    playfulness, his pranks,
His driving you through mud—
    a badly marked provincial road—
Looking for something, he didn't know what,
    and sinking you up to the hubcaps,
And how you saw it then:
    the spring fields, the splendour.

I never wrote that poem.
    I wrote down words—none of them mine—
That ought to count for more:
    the Russian *Zhizneradostny*,
Which isn't "cheerful" or "joyous",
    but even better: "life-glad."
From Brecht I wrote down *Freundlichkeit*,
    from Chaucer: *Gentilesse*.

Ah, Toby, what a thing to ask me.
    To write a poem about your husband,
Dead from cancer, whom I never really knew.
    And you were perfectly serious,

Wondering: couldn't I catch something
of his life?
You'd tell me stories, give me the details:
for he was life-glad and gentle,
He was kind....

In a hall at Aldeburgh an attentive audience is
momentarily distracted by the jet (American—
The base hasn't moved very far) which flies above them
as they listen to a song by Britten
Or by Gustav Holst. Where Thomas Hardy prayed
(dismaying Clodd, his scientific friend),
Where George Crabbe's father preached,
is space, is history made soluble in art,
A good man's life made durable? Cynouai is bored,
Laura is tired. As the plane approaches,
Both of them look up. If they could understand;
If I could let them know.

Oh, I remember you that day: the terror in
your face, the irony and love. And I remember
What you wanted me to do. That ancient charge: to
read whatever evidence in lives or lies appears,
In stones or bells—transform, transfigure then whatever
comedy, catastrophe or crime, and thus
Return the earth, thus redeem the time. And this:
to leave it all alone (unspoken always: look, I have
This moment and this place): *Cum on, cum on my owyn
swet chyld; goo we hom and take owr rest...*
Sing we to the oldest harpe, and playe.... Old friend,
old debt: I'm welcoming at last your presence now.
I'm but half-oriented here. I'm digging down.

3
from *Crossing*

Dunwich: Winter Visit Alone

for Diana

> *"There is presence in what is missing; there is*
> *history in there being so little..."* —Henry James

Younger & younger, we were married here
Where cliffs fall into the sea
And most of the village has
Disappeared, drowning in its leas.
I have not loved you less for that.

And if it is chastening to know
That fishermen catch
Their nets on the bell-towers,
Sunken and singing,
I have not loved you less for that,

Even though I have not loved you
As I might have, if, merchant
Or seaman, I had come here with you
To a safe coast in a good time.
No, I have not loved you less for that.

And knowing well the presences here
From the start, and of absence,
Of history alive, still, in so little,
We face the tides and erosions.
And I will not love you less for that.

No, I will not love you less for that.

Two Ladies

I

So many incorrupt bodies, such
Corrupting times!
Edmund to and fro for years,

Inspected, found intact,
Unburied & unbothered & unblemished
And then, then these ladies

These incorruptible ladies
Like Etheldreda Queen & Sainted Audrey
Earlier than Edmund even

Wearing round her neck a fabled string
Of beads that purpled flesh
Into a fatal tumor that she liked:

She had, she said, been vain.
Daughter of the hypothetical incumbent
Of the ship at Sutton Hoo,

Daughter of the priest who taught her,
Touchy and untouched—
By Tondbert Prince of Fenmen and

By Ecgfrith son of Osway the Northumbrian—
She ruled, queened, twice,
And got sick of it, of royalty, and fled:

Fled to Abbess Eba, solicitous and grave,
Where randy Ecgfrith followed
With his louts who'd leered at her around

The smutty fire inside the great log hall.
Flowering near Ely
Among fowlers, among fishermen & fogs—& bogs—

Famously her pilgrim's staff took root
& that was Etheldreda's Stow.
They say in Etheldreda's Stow today, they *say*—

That water bubbling from her temporary grave
Was Audrey's Spring: & any bauble
There that's worn around the neck's called tawdry.

II

Margery Kempe from Lynn
Would howl and wail "full plenteously"
When told of mirth & pleasures

"Full boisterously" she sobbed
Who was no Wycliffite or Lollard but
Could censure equally

Some bumpkin local reprobate or mighty
Philip Repington and
Greater Arundel upon his Bishop's throne.

Full plenteously, full boisterously
She'd wail: full homely, too!
She was her own Salvation Army band

And drummed and trumpeted vulgarity that
Such as Chesterton would
Understand to be an efficacious pastorale.

Some amanuensis took it down, our first
Biography—be glad! *She* was:
Of plenteous continual weeping by a creature

Who would be the bride of Christ, a pilgrim pure
And not the failed brewer, failed
Miller married to the borough chamberlain

John Kempe that she, said citizens of Lynn,
Pretty clearly was. Contentious;
Weird; she sailed away. The Mamelukes

And Saracens were less impressed with her
Outside the Holy Sepulchre
Than those who'd suffered her for weeks

On board the ship. Said one: a vexèd spirit.
Another: that she'd surfeited on wine.
A third that surely fatal illnesses came on

Like that: *O put her in a heavy sea*
O put her in a little boat
Without a bottom O. Thus, Amanuensis says,

Had each his thoughts. At
York, at Cawood Palace, the Archbishop:
"Woman!—Why, why

Then weepest thou?" And Margery: *Sir, ye*
Shall wish some day
That ye had wept as sore as I!

Verrucas

The solemn doctor, eyeing painfully
My six verrucas,
Closed the heavy office door—

Well, he said, *we often find in fact*
The skinman doesn't
Do much good, his acids

And his sparks, they
All come back—these warts—
And so we usually

Suggest—and you Americans
Are shocked—
(He looked behind him then)

The local witch. The what?
That's right, he said.
I drove a mile or two and found

Her house. A white witch, certainly,
She smiled a kindly smile
& smoked a caked & gnarled briar pipe.

She counted up verrucas, multiplied,
And tied her knots
In just as many strings

As she would bury, burn, or bless.
I used to use a hunk
Of steak for skin disease, she said,

The method's good. I'd slap
It on a warty cheek or sole, and that
Was that. But what with

Meat so dear and all—you'll understand
We don't use mince! this hex'll
Work for you, all right. Three days!

She packed me hobbling off
& said a spell. I tossed a silver coin
In the bottom of her well.

After the Death of Chekhov

for Bob Hass

Anton Pavlovitch has died
At Badenweiler, a spa
Where doctors had sent him,

A doctor, with his beautiful Olga.
They ship the body to Moscow
Where both of us wait at the station.

This is the difference between us:
You, with Chaliapin & Gorki,
Calm the disorderly crowd

And stick with your man: You
Go off in the proper direction
And weep at the grave of the poet,

While I get confused,
Follow a band of the Tzar's
Which is playing a march

In the cortège of a general
Killed in the Japanese War.
Or, when the two coffins arrive

At the platform together,
One in a car labeled
Oysters, and you understand in

A flash which one is Chekhov's,
This is the difference between us:
You return to your wife and honor

The dead by telling hilarious jokes
About Chaliapin and Gorki, while I am sent
To a spa in the car labeled *Oysters*.

You Measure John

for Diana, at work in the Fitzwilliam

For posterity you measure John.
For the catalogue
you measure with a tape
his works
and recognize yourself as woman
among women
in the life of this man John, his death.

You measure for the catalogue
the pictures
and their frames
thinking of the others
measuring his need
measuring his pride (who could not
please himself)
measuring his gypsy caravans of children
as he went away to paint, badly,
the famous and the rich.

No, you do not like Augustus John.
Measuring the thickness
of a new biography you offer me
I think—
not. You tell it simply
and with no embellishments yourself.
It is an old story:
some man damages the lives of women
who would love him.
There are various excuses.
One is art.

Mark Twain in the Fens

i

Not the trip of 1872
when fame first fanned an Anglophilia
and glory burst from every side
upon him—
And not the trip of 1879
when he howled for *real coffee,*
corn bread, good roast beef
with taste to it.

The last trip; the exile & the debts.

Thish-yer Smiley had a yeller
one-eyed cow that didn't have no tail....
At Brandon Creek, Ship Inn.
They bring him real coffee, good
roast beef with taste to it.

ii

　　　　　　　Recently got up
by him as Joan of Arc,
his eldest daughter once had fled
the Bryn Mawr auditorium—
meningitis all but creeping
up her spine—

He told them all a tingler,
having sworn to her he wouldn't,
called *The Golden Arm.*

　　　Death made real by hers?
and deathless tales
a part of blame? My *fault, my fault*—
And this: *I'll pay*

though still he dreams each night
about his miracle-working
machine, the Paige Typesetter,
his Dark Angel of print.

   iii

*Thish-yer Smiley had a yeller
one-eyed cow that didn't have no tail....*

No one writes it down
or sets it up in type. It is the last
he is going to tell.

It is all over with him. It's
begun. All night long
he tells and tells and tells.

Paul Verlaine in Lincolnshire

i

For a while he had that famous friendship.
But what's inspired debauchery
and manic vision
to illuminations from the English hymnal?
Keble's stanzas? Wesley's? Stanzas
by good Bishop Ken?
Ô mon Dieu, vous m'avez blessé d'amour.

For indulgence, there was Tennyson.
He walked to Boston from the grammar school
in Stickney to confess.

ii

And wrote *Sagesse* there in Lincolnshire.
And went to chapel,
and taught the ugly boys finesse.
He had been condemned to death,
he boasted, in the Siege
of Paris...
        Colonel Grantham and
the credulous headmaster
listened to the story
of his clever rescue by Thiers....

Even in the hands of Debussy, Fauré,
the Catholic *lied* Verlainian would sing
the strangest nonconformist airs.

Ô mon Dieu, vous m'avez blessé d'amour.

And to proper Mallarmé he wrote
about the absinthe: *I'd still take it*
with sugar....
The school record books
do not suggest
that he excelled at rugger.

O there were many rhymes—
But he was on his best behavior,
pious, calm, bourgeois.
The peaceful English countryside
acted on his conscience
like a rudder.

Ô mon Dieu, vous m'avez blessé d'amour.

Lines for the Gentlemen

i

1667. And on Landguard beach, 1000 Dutch.
That was the last invasion.
Afterwards, 1753-66,
Governor Thicknesse, thank you, defending, sir.
(And plenty of out-of-work sailors)

ii

And as with piracy, there's honour in it.
And not just honour among thieves—
A rising class will not, they'd tell you,
be put down. Custom?
                        Brandy! tea, wool, rum,
just name it—
So the word gets round. Someone's
had the pox, someone's
had the plague. All's free trade
at certain cottages where rumoured illnesses
or rumoured ghosts
keep all but customers away—

Laces for a lady; letters for a spy
And watch the wall, my darling, while the
        Gentlemen go by.

iii

This one watched the wall; that one
closed his eyes.
The headless gunner walked on the embankment.

A crescent moon rose smartly from behind
the nasty gibbet. There are
voices in the back room of The Crown—

and Mr Plumer, MP from Appleby,
speaking in the House
and saying ALL IMPROVEMENT OF THE LAND

HAS BEEN SUSPENDED
while the Parson whispers to his wife
the wages of gin

for our duties
and hides the three enormous tubs
beneath the altar cloth.

4,000,000 gallons of booze are flowing
into England! (Three slow
cutters chasing one fast swipe.)

The publican
has put the spotsmen all to sleep.
Bright lights are flashing

down the Orwell and the Alde.

From a Visit to Dalmatia

   i

Korčula is oleander, cypresses & twisted
fig trees; Korčula is stones—
Lemon trees and stones. Quick mirages
above the stones & olive groves:
Shaky vineyard walls of broken stones and

Stones that must be gathered, piled up
before the shallow arbor roots will
take a tenuous hold
in sandy earth: And shallow stony graves
for Partisan or priest, invader.

Limestone & limestone rock in hills
around Lumbarda, limeface of Sveti Ilija
after Orebić:
            Rockslides and
washed out roads, karst—
a landscape that will break you on its back
or make a sculptor of you—

Lozica, Kršinić, Ivan Jurjević-Knez.

   ii

Or if not a sculptor then a fisherman.
Or, it would have once.
            Looking at the empty streets
at noon, Toni Bernidić
tells me it's the woist and hottest
day so far in June—he learned
his English in Brooklyn
during the war—
But his house is cool, and so
are the wines: Grk, Pošip, Dingač....

He tells me of the wooden ships
he built, each one taking
him a year: but well made, well made—
The work, he says,
was heavy—pointing to his tools.

Now he has no work: the island's
income is from tourists
and the flushed young men who'd once
have been apprentices
sport their *Atlas* badges, ride their
scooters to the Park or Marco Polo
or the Bon Repos
and show their muscles to the breezy
blue-eyed girls
whose wealthy fathers order loudly
wiener schnitzel

wienerschnitzel and stones.

Friendship

One day I do you a good turn. Then
You do me *two* good turns.
I am pleased by that & say so the next day.

You break the lead in your pencil.
I loan you mine.
You give me an expensive fountain pen.

I play you a recording of The Modern Jazz Quartet.
Though you like Milt Jackson's vibes, you
Take me to *The Ring* at Covent Garden after which

We introduce each other to our wives.
My wife teaches your wife how to cook fondues.
Your wife teaches my wife how to live.

I dedicate my book to you & you are moved.
You make a character of me in yours:
It is singled out for praise by the reviewers.

I give my mistress to your loyalest disciple.
Claiming he is bored with her, you have
The wench returned; her skills are much improved.

When I sing my secret lute song about mountains,
You take me to the mountains
In your car: You have a cabin there

Where after drinks we agree to a primitive contest.
Preparing for it, you
Scar your face grotesquely with a razor blade.

Upon return, I burn for you my manuscript.
For me you smash your files. I wreck my mother's house.
You wreck your only daughter's mind.

In the end, I write a letter saying:
I forgive you. But you do not write back.
It is now the time for silence.

For we are friends. We love each other very much.

Brandon, Breckland: The Flint Knappers

(after a chapter in Julian Tennyson's Suffolk Scene*)*

The Forestry Commission was about to plant
the Breckland on the day young Julian Tennyson

visited the Edwardses, last knappers of Brandon.
Because some tribes in Central Africa

hadn't heard about percussion caps
there still was business for the craftsmen

that supplied the flint for Wellington
and watched the plovers & the curlews dip at home.

Alien, the Breckland seemed as sinister & desolate
to Tennyson as 1938, the stark flint cottages

all shining darkly in reflecting pools
of stone and dusty sorrel, riding in the ragwort

and the bugloss, or jutting out of bracken,
heather, thin brown grass.

Wheatears, stonechats, whinchats, pipits—
all in the same still air—

and Julian, once a Suffolk countryman's Huck Finn,
feeling terrors coming on him

now at twenty-three, feeling *loosed in some
primeval, flat and limitless arena—*

leagues and leagues and leagues of it, he wrote,
severed from the rest of England.

Brandon on the Little Ouse was a relief from that,
though still in Breckland.

Malting, watermeadows, fine old bridge—
as lovely a corner as any I have found in Suffolk.

The elder Edwards, coughing, takes him
in his workshop, shuts the door, and points:

topstone, wallstone, floorstone chips
from Lingheath Common quarry, ornaments & tinders,

flints for muskets, carbines, pistols—
quartered first, then flaked and knapped with

pointed hammer on a flattened rod of iron.
When the headmen learn about percussion caps

the show's all over, Edwards said.
And anyway we've not got one apprentice

and the quarrier's retired. It would die with him,
his art, these mysteries of Breckland.

Meanwhile Tennyson looks on amazed
as Edwards bevels edges, hammers, hammers, talks:

I did it on the radio into a microphone, I
did it on the BBC before the news.

There are reports. Off in Central Africa
sprawls a man who feels of a sudden loosed in some

primeval flat and limitless arena—
leagues and leagues and leagues of it, he thinks

in his delirium. There is a flight of birds.
On Berner's green: an Air Ministry bombing-ground;

here the Forestry Commission will plant firs.
Badgers and foxes, jays and crows

will populate the land the curlews flee, *and when
the Old Guard fell before great Wellington*

England sang the knappers of the Brandon flints!
It is the year of Munich. Tennyson will die

in Burma from a piece of shrapnel the size of any
smallish hag-stone he'd have found

among discarded chips on Edwards' dusty floor
and which his copy of George Borrow

pressing pages from a manuscript of *In Memoriam*
will not deflect. Reflected in his book,

an Indian summer. Ice will one day lift
the Blaxhall Stone itself as far as Brandon moor.

59 Lines Assembled Quickly
Sitting on a Wall Near the Reconstruction
of the Lady Juliana's Cell

Heavily   heavily
hidden away—

the door is
barred & barred   and

singing
veni creator

spiritus   "a service
of Enclosure"

& the cell
is consecrated

and the door
is barred   and

singing
veni creator

spiritus you have
a window on

the church you have
a window on

the world
and appearances

and revel-
ations   visions!

"showings"
to a soul *that*

cowde
no letter: cowde—

could, cloud
no cloud or cold

unknowing sin
is what

there loud? or
quiet sin is what

behoved? or is
behovable

il convient que
le péché

existe: le péché is
serviceable

what is
an anchorhold what is

an anchoress
the Lady Juliana's

one re-
corded visit from the

frenzied Margerie Kempe
as praise

& praise & gesture
I prefer

to Juliana's
Kemp's

the *other* Kemp's
Will Kemp's

who Morris-danced
from London

days   on days
from London

Kemp's who
lept!   immortally

this Norwich wall

26 June 1381/1977

I NORTH WALSHAM: THE FIELDS

And he, Despenser, tried to keep hold
Of the dyer's head

As the crowd of them, gawkers
& priests, tinkers & tailors & wastrels

(Gentry too, thinking already: *reredos!*
A gift for him, a

Presentiment) lurched along
With the horsecart off to the place

Of undoing, Lidster's undoing who'd heard—
Who'd heard of *The Kynges*

Son who'd paye for al,
The mullere who'd ygrounde smal—but

Was paying himself,
Tied by a foot with the same rope

That they'd hang him with, after
The drawing. And he

Henry Despenser, the Bishop "Lespenser"—
miles amatus, boni pastoris mens,

For so it says on his brass—
Hopping behind the cart like a toad,

The cart they dragged the dyer behind
For that was the law:

To be dragged to the place of undoing.
This, however, was extra:

The Bishop himself coddling your head
In his skirts

And you "The King of the Commons",
"The Idol of Norfolk"

Whose bell had been rung
By Ball and Tyler and Straw. Oh

This dispenser of justice was special,
sui generis the man who

Had caught you, tried you, confessed you,
The man who would hang you

See you in quarters, one for each of
The earth's: hopping

Behind the cart like a toad...
And reaching out for your head   which

Aoi!   he'd drop on a cobble a cobble
a cobble and *there*

Then catch it up again, mother it back
In his apron, your head

Like an apple or melon or globe. Where,
Where did you travel, where

Did you think you could go—
The two of you, then, staff, of one, life?

II St Luke's Chapel, Norwich Cathedral

We look at the reredos, the retables.
Of course the "subject"

Is "Christ"…. But the blood & the power
That steadied the hand

And shook the knees and the wits of the
Master from Norwich—*that*

Was the blood and the power of Dyer
And Bishop, of Lidster

And Henry Despenser. Behind me somebody
Mumbles the word *chiliastic.*

His fellow-tourist says, looking hard: it's
Absolutely fantastic!

The five panels escaped the smashings
Of Cromwell. The five

Scenes from the Passion here are restored.
And we may embrace

The arcana, study
The photomicrographic specifics:

A patient lady explains: *malachite,*
Azurite: And the head of Christ is restored!

The rotten wood is restored: the order
Is restored. *Israelite,*

Trotskyite. Edmund Burke said of the famous
Rhyme: *it rhymes!* And also: *a sapient*

Maxim: When Adam delved and Eve span, who
Was then the gentle man?

Nobody knows what Lidster said, but that's
What he heard: *The Kynges son schal*

Paye for al
The mullere hath ygrounde smal—and

Paid it himself,
Tied by a foot with the same rope

They'd etcetera. *Spin*:
The painting and the restoration

Are brilliantly done. *Delve*: the revolt
Alas was untimely—even Engels

Would say so—and Henry Despenser's work
Was brilliantly done—

And us with our heads still on our necks?
With books in our laps,

Stupid or giddy, gawking—
Us with the eyes still in their sockets

And tongues still in our mouths—
Where do we travel, where

Do we think we can go—
All of us, now, staff, of one, life?

On the Death of Benjamin Britten

Operas! A feast for burghers, said Adorno.
And of your work: The apotheosis
Of meagerness, a kind of fast. That's
A cruel case against you
And it may have weight, in time.
But let's call meagerness
Economy today
And call the bourgeoisie the people
Who like me have (barely) what it costs
To listen and who like to hear
These songs, but who will pay a price.
Economies of living soon enough
Make meager even music of the spheres!
To be of use, you said.
Directly and deliberately I write
For human beings. And not
Posterity—for which the general outlook
Isn't very bright.

A tenor mourns. And you lie down in Aldeburgh
One last time. But you have work to do
In spite of what the two of us have said.
A tenor sings. When you
Get out there over the horizon
This December morning with the likes
Of Peter Grimes,
Row your shining boat ashore
And be extravagant in song:
Leave economy to the ungrateful living
Who will need it, whose Justice
And whose History have multiplied unendingly
Expenses by Apotheoses by Sublimes.

Poem for Cynouai

I

With urgency and passion you argue for the lot—
every one of thirty watercolors
ranged in retrospective
which I thought to choose among.
Circumspect, I sought
negotiations. You squint your lazy eye
and wave your arm in arcs
around our geocentric circle and insist:
"We'll take them all!"

II

I am easily persuaded.
How luminous their rendering of a world
we both believe in
and can sometimes share:—
where names are properties of things
they name, where stones
are animate and wilful, trees
cry out in storms, and compulsive
repetition of the efficacious formulae
will get us each his way.

When they patched your overcompensating eye
your work began. Your starboard
hemisphere was starved for colors
and for shapes.
Suddenly a punning and holistic
gnostic, you painted
everything in sight:
your left eye flashed at cats & camels
in the clouds, while one by one
you drew them with a shrewd right hand

into a white corral.
At school they said your "problem"
was "perceptual".

III

What did you perceive,
and what did I?
I found that scattering of words
in notes. I wrote it down
two years ago and now you do not paint.
I no longer wrote. It's out
of date, we've changed.
I was going to quote Piaget
and go on to talk about perception.
Instead I went to work
and earned some money, girl.
I was going to call
you *child.*

Two years, then. We'll keep it honest
as I wander back with you
to Shelford. Bob & Earlene live in Shelford
now, Leif and Luke and Kristin.
Bob has poems in which
he whispers *child, child.*
"We'll take them all", you said,
and I said
I am easily persuaded.
We took just one.

IV

But it is altogether marvelous.
I've kept it here while
you've gone riding with your friends.
Your passion now is horses.
It feels as if you've been away two years—

two years.
Stout-hearted Moshe,
peering one-eyed through your
horse's ears, this bright Ikon that
you've left me makes me
think of William Blake's *Glad Day.*
One sad poet wrote: My
daughter's heavier. And another:
O may she be beautiful, but
not *that* beautiful. I have a friend
who's visited Ms Yeats—
She's bald with warts! O daughters
and their bright glad days
growing beautiful or heavier or bald.
O foolish leers and Lears.

We played. And we play now, but
not so much. Our problem
was perceptual. I think we were
perhaps too Japanese:
I have it on authority
that formal speech retains
the spirit of *bushido* in Japan.
In the *asobase-Kotoba*
we don't say: "I'm here in Shelford"
or "You're riding"
but: "I pretend to be in Shelford"
and "You play at
going riding." Nor does one say:
"I hear your father's dead",
but this instead:
"I understand your father
has played dying."

V

When my father finished playing dying
I began.
You gave me pictures
which I held against a wound.
I wrote: "How luminous their rendering
of a world we both believe in"
and then I think you stopped believing....

For money, with a friend,
I helped to translate Lars Norén
who far away
in dark, cold Sweden wrote:

Today I see that my daughter
is higher, greater
than I, and completed... Her
hard kaiser head encircles me & carries
me and helps me. Silently
we speak in each other—Then
she paves the dead ones.
She comes towards me in her kaiser skirt.

How I stumbled after you with memories & books.
How far ahead you rode. How very
quickly all the books
were closed. How frightening the horses are

As you approach me on The Black Duke of Norfolk.
The Duke's Funeral Helm is low on your eyes
(I stole it for you from a golden nail
in Framlingham church).
Your Ming Dynasty jodhpurs cling to your legs,
cling to your horse's sides
(I sent for them express to Rajasthan).
Your Dalai Lama coat is zipped up tight
(I zipped it up myself).
Your green Tzarina vest divests me.

Your beady Pony Club badge is a third eye
pinned to your cheating heart.
On a velvet photograph of Princess Anne
you are riding in circles of dust.
One eye is patched, old pirate,
and the other eye is glazed.
Only the third one, the Pony Club badge,
can see me, and it stares,
fiery and triumphant.
You are riding in circles of dust.
You are riding into the eye of the Pony Club badge.

First they patched your eye
and then I saw.
My problem was perceptual.

Lars Norén concludes:
She hungers after herself....

VI

What I had wanted to say was: *red, ocher,
orange, blue, green, violet.*
What I had wanted to say was: *grass, sky,
sun, moon, child, forest, sea.*
I had wanted to say: *English village.*
I had wanted to say:
English village a long time ago....
What I had wanted to hear
was the music of flutes and recorders
in a summer garden—
flutes and recorders and tambourines....

What I had wanted to see was light
filtering through the trees
deep in a forest near the sea
where elves and children play together
and adults sip tea
by an enormous ornamented samovar

112

in solemn conversation
on the nature of the games
the elves & children play....
What I had wanted to write was
love, immortal, laughter, wings....
What I had wanted to do
was to walk forever into a vision
painted by my daughter.
I had wanted her to take me with her there.
I had wanted her
to close the door behind us....

VII

Made of blues and ochers, greens,
made of sunrise and of grass & sky & trees—
Which will be the day
that you remember, child,
when I am only soul-stuff
and can no more enjoy this awkward body
which, despite its ills,
manages to do extraordinary simple things
like walk through heaths of gorse
with you before the others are awake
as the sun comes over
the edge of the earth the ships fall off of
as they tilt on their keels
and roll on the world's last wave....

I remember a day: the rowboat rocked
in the reeds:
my father watched his line. All
the night before we had slept together
in a shack waiting for the dawn.
We didn't talk for hours. He, for once,
was beautifully distracted from
what he always called "the difficult business
of living." There was
no past, there was no future there

in those reeds...
                    we were adrift in time,
in timelessness
and no one said we must return—

nor did we sail over any edge of any earth.

Or again: near the house of my childhood
on a street called Glen Echo Drive
there was a tree, an oak,
where my father swung me in a swing—
his long thin fingers
and his firm damp palms on the small of my back
I feel still—
and my bare & grimy feet going up through the leaves!

Mosses grow between his fingers now
and along his palms.
Mosses grow in his mouth & under his arms.
When he finished playing dying
I began....
You gave me pictures
which I held against a wound.
I wrote: *How luminous their rendering* as

You came toward me saying *muzzle, poll, crest,*
withers, loins, croup, dock...
As you came saying *snaffle, whip, spurs,*
pommel, cantle, girth.

VIII

And so I try to learn new words
like any child—
I say *flank, hock, heel, hoof;*
I say *fetlock, gaskin, thigh, stifle, sheath.*
I would meet you now
according to my bond. I try to put away
this Ikon which sustained me.

I write *Equitation: Mounting & dismounting.*
Circumspect, I seek
negotiations. I wave my arms
around in frantic circles and insist:
"I'll learn them all"
while you ride off on paths
through fields of gorse and into sunsets
which are not even slightly picturesque—

While you ride off in hurricanes of dust.

—Just one time were three of us together:
father, father-son, and daughter.
We played at something, riding, painting,
poetry, or dying—
it hardly matters what...
And at our playing
                    —(while, perhaps,
someone picked a mandolin
and strangers talked about us solemnly
around an ornamented samovar
and sipped their tea)—
our lines of vision crossed
and then we started changing places painfully....

The child is father of the man
but not the child the poet meant.
The child of flesh and blood
and not the ghost of former selves
is father of the man—
The Daughter on the Black Duke of Norfolk
She
is father of the man
The Daughter
Who is Higher, Greater & Completed
She
is father of the man
The Daughter on the Black Duke of Norfolk
The one who made the picture
the one who gave the gift

the one who paved the dead
the one who wore the patch
the one who was Japanese
the one who learned to ride a horse
And Hungers After Herself—

She
is father of the man
The daughter on the Black Duke of Norfolk

The one whose problem was perceptual

The one who rides away

> And the Manual says: *It is interesting to assess the progress and accuracy of the training by riding a circle on ground upon which the imprints of the horse's hoofs can be seen....*

(1974-1977)

4

Translations, Imitations, Dedications

After Ekelöf

for Göran Printz-Påhlson

I broke off a branch from
A thin, young tree
Leaving an eye-knot, an eye

It watched as I thrashed
A young bride
On a coast way up in the north

I slept for five hundred years

By a great felled tree
I awoke
On a coast way up in the north

I polished a piece of the thick-veined wood
And over an eye-knot
I painted the face of a mother

August

1

The stones are hot.
The cattle are lowing.
The long-clothed infants flutter down
With a drop of milk in their mouths.
The smoke billows,
Dense pleated smoke
Or the thin flesh
Which rises still,
Smoke from unused honey
Or smoke from fires in trees,
It rises,
It brings down the subterraneans.

2

Girls and dogs
Sleep in the grass
Life is
A heartbeat
From my own
      The burning cattle
With tonsured skulls
Have come home
To their quivering stable.

3

Today I see that my daughter
Is higher, greater
Than I, and completed... Her
Hard Kaiser head encircles me and carries
Me and helps me. We speak
Silently in each other and then
She paves the dead ones.
> She comes towards me in her Kaiser skirt.

From the crib of the road
In a dust cloud of sleeping crickets,
Her large blue eyes are watching
How the realm of day binds its book.
> She hungers after herself.

*translated with Göran Printz-Påhlson
from the Swedish of Lars Norén*

'Void which falls out of void...'

a

Void which falls out of void, transparent,
cones, hemispheres,
fall through empty space.
Thoughtform, crescent, trajectory.

b

However relevant!
In the infinite freedom I can
keep back, give
my notes resilience, in relation
to each other, to my whole body, which also
falls in infinity through empty space:
e.g.
Charlie Parker's solo in *Night in Tunisia* on May 15th 1953.

c

The flight of sentimentality through empty space.
Through its elliptical hole
an heraldic blackbird's
black wings, yellow beak, round eyes, with the yellow
ring, which defines its inner empty
space.

*translated with Göran Printz-Påhlson
from the Swedish of Göran Sonnevi*

Free Translation and Recombination:
Fragments from Octavio Paz

"No ví girar las formas hasta desvanecerse
En claridad inmóvil..."

*

By negation is my increase, my wealth.
Lord, Lord of erosions and dispersions,
I come to you in the whirlwind.

Into the oldest tree I drive my nail.

*

In the architecture of silence
Is no debate between the bees
And the statistics.

Nor is there any dialectic among apes.

The wind blows. The rain obliterates
The mason's mark. On every psalm (on every
Mask of lime) a crown of fire appears.

*

To rattle semantic seeds:
To bury the word, the kernel of fire,
In the body of Ceres:

　　　poem, poem

Spilling the water and wine,
Spilling the fire.

*

Shake the book like a branch,
Detaching a phrase:

Voices and laughter,
Dancing and tambourines.

This is the winter solstice,
Who will awaken the stones?

Shake the book, detaching a word:
Pollywog, poison, periwig...

Say it: a penance of words.

*

But the huddled men in the alleys,
The huddled men in the squares & the mosques,
They took my gems and my grave-clothes.

I was covered with poems.

In the center of incandescence,
In the column of noon,
I was ringed with sand and insomnia.

I was covered with poems.

*

And the sophistry of clocks.
And the provinces of abstract towns.

Dizzy geometries, vertigoes.

Not to foretell but to tell.
To say it: a paring away.

Nombre Antiguo del Fuego

    in the tunnels of onyx
      the circles of salt,
   chimerical child of
     calculus and of thirst:

From every stone appears a brief black tongue
Naming the scales of the night.

Agape

(after the poem by César Vallejo)

I won't say anyone comes here and asks.
They haven't this afternoon
Asked me for anything much. Nothing!

Not one leper presented himself.
I haven't today
Kissed my quota of sores.

In so fine a parading of lights, I haven't
Seen a single burial flower.
Lord, Lord: I've died so little today,

I'm sorry, forgive me. Everybody goes by
But nobody asks for a thing.
Mal, mal in my hands, like a *cosa ajena.*

If you've mislaid it it's here!
Well, I've gone to the door & I've shouted.
How many doors get slammed in my face!

Something *ajeno ajeno* roots in my soul
And I don't tell you somebody comes here & asks.
Lord, Lord: I've died so little today.

To V.V.: On Our Translation of the Kossovo Fragments

Vladeta the Voyvoda!
>   knight who brings the news
From Kossovo
>   to gracious Militsa,
Lazarus's queen,
>   sister of the Jugovici,
Daughter of Jug Bogdan—
>   that's the stock you're made of!
In the name
>   of God Almighty
As they all repeat
>   in these old epic poems
We struggle with
>   (and even in the name
Of Allah maybe)
>   what could ever bring
A hero and a Serb
>   to South Bend, Indiana?

Where Ivan Mestrović
>   petered out his talent
In the awful portrait busts
>   and bland madonnas
Of his exile
>   we meet beside
The only decent
>   piece of work in town—
His "Jacob's Well"
>   and puzzle over
Fates as dark
>   as those of Lazarus
And Milosh Obilitch
>   sung down centuries
Of Turkish occupation
>   by dusty peasant guslers

Who didn't need to know
              that fancy alphabet
Saint Cyril left behind,
              in which reforming Vuk
Spelled out phonetically
              a living language
Where one itches through
              the final syllables of names
And scratches at the surface
              of a destiny
In verbal fragments
              of a people's epic past.

How unlikely, Vladeta,
              that we should meet at all.
In 1941 when I was born
              beside a silly field
Of vegetables
              that noncombatant types
Were urged to cultivate—
              officially they called
Such doubtful husbandry
              a "Victory Garden"—
You at just eighteen
              had taken to the hills
With Tito's partisans
              where every urgent message
Sent to Stalin
              (later on to Churchill)
Was the same:
              More boots!
The rugged karst
              that cut away your soles
Kept "the occupier",
              as the euphemistic
Tour books call him now
              (for, after all, he's rich),
An easy target
              in the villages & towns.

Did you swoop right down on him
                    like Marko on the Turks?
You did—
                    but couldn't live with
Certain knowledge
                    of unspeakable reprisals.
Nazi mathematics was
                    a good deal easier
To follow than your theory
                    of recursive functions
Hammered out in hiding
                    six months later in Vienna—
For every officer
                    you blew up in the town
They shot
                    a hundred villagers.
And who is more
                    within his rights
To moralize on firing squads
                    than someone who himself
Would stand before one—
                    Trying you summarily, your
Brothers tied you to a tree
                    and lined up in a nasty file
With leveled rifles aimed
                    to blow your very useful brains
To far less squeamish hills.

You can laugh four decades later
                    since you've lived to tell
The tale:
                    "But my uncle, who as fate
Would have it is in charge
                    of this grim liquidation,
Couldn't shoot his nephew.
                    That was 1941: two years later
And he would have."
                    He cut you loose and kicked
You in the ass
                    and shouted: *Run!*

In the ballad, Vladeta
                survives to tell the queen
What he saw at Kossovo:
                "Tell me knight," she says,
"When you were on
                that wide and level plain
Did you see
                great Lazar riding by?
Did you see my father
                and my noble brothers there?
Did you see the husbands
                of my daughters?"
And Vladeta must tell
                of slaughter and betrayal
—the gusler singing
                mournfully in lines of just
Ten syllables, sliding over
                pauses at the fourth
Where prosodists
                would quickly place
Twin horizontal lines—
                Yes, Vladeta must tell
The queen exactly what
                annihilation feels like.

That I see you sometimes
                standing among memories
Like this other Vladeta
                before the queen
Or Mestrović
                among his early works
Or even like Lord Milosh
                on that open plain
You find, of course,
                unspeakably absurd—
"With my broken
                battle lance, no doubt,
As all the enemy
                press in upon me fighting

Near the river Sitnitsa.
                    One account says Milosh
Killed twelve thousand
                    Turkish soldiers after
He had polished off
                    the Sultan. In fact they
Took him in the tent and
                    cut off both his arms!"

You open up the slivovitz
                    and go on with your tales—
Which, my friend, for all
                    the jokes and ironies
Required for the telling
                    never cease to bleed—
And in your cups you sing
                    to me Prince Lazar's fatal choice,
You sing the ancient
                    downfall of the Serbs.
"Which Kingdom is it
                    that you long for most?
That's the question that
                    the falcon asked the Tzar.
If you choose the earth, he said,
                    then saddle horses,
Tighten girths—
                    have your knights put on
Their swords and make
                    a dawn attack against
The Turks: your enemy
                    will be destroyed.
But if you choose the skies
                    then build a church—
Oh, not of stone
                    but out of silk and velvet—
Gather up your forces,
                    take the bread and wine,
For all shall perish,
                    perish utterly,

And you, O Tzar,
　　　　　shall perish with them."

As you break your words
　　　　　for our inadequate exchange
And give me phrases which
　　　　　in token of their real worth
I give you back in scribbled
　　　　　& devalued English notes
I hear you choose the earth
　　　　　even as you tell me otherwise
And laughingly declare:
　　　　　The skies, the skies!
For you are out there
　　　　　on that wide & level plain;
You see yourself
　　　　　great Lazar riding by;
You see the father
　　　　　of the Lady's brothers there;
You see the husbands
　　　　　of her daughters—
And when your uncle
　　　　　cuts you loose
You stumble
　　　　　through the villages & hills
Playing tokens
　　　　　for survival, whispering
In code to border guards
　　　　　& agents, prostitutes & poets,
Fellow travelers and
　　　　　their wealthy following
Of contraband tobacconists
　　　　　an anagram compounded
Of the talismanic words
　　　　　that wound the clocks
In old Regusa:
　　　　　OBLITI PRIVATORUM
PUBLICA CURATE—
　　　　　Forget your private business

And concern yourself
        with public life, that's
The gist of it—
        knowing well that only those
A man can trust will whisper
        the correct response.
For if a man's a friend
        he knows that underneath
Those proudly chiseled words
        above the lintel close beside
The Rector's palace
        there's a dusty little shop
Whose owner chalks
        (in lingua franca too!)
Upon a blackboard
        hanging in his narrow window
The reply:
        ANYTIME FRIED FISHES.
And that's the phrase,
        you tell me, answers Latin.
That's the phrase
        that took you underground!
Obliti Privatorum Publica Curate
        you intone, and I cry out:
Anytime Fried Fishes!
        and we hug each other like
Two drunken Slavs
        and weep like sentimental
Irishmen & leave our
        empty bottle on the pedestal
Of Mestrović's well.

Vladeta, my Voyvoda,
        my dear unhappy friend,
There is no Kingdom
        left for us to choose—
Neither of the earth
        nor of the sky.
But peace, peace,
        to all who wander

For whatever reason
        from their stony lands
Bringing all the heavy cargo
        of their legends
Humming in a cipher
        in their lucid, spinning minds!

The Kossovo Maiden

On a Sunday
                    early in the morning
The Maid of Kossovo
                    awoke to brilliant sun
And rolled her sleeves
                    above her snow-white elbows;

On her back she carries
                    fresh, warm bread,
And in her hands she bears
                    two golden goblets,
One of water,
                    one of dark red wine.
Seeking out
                    the plain of Kossovo,
She walks upon the field
                    of slaughter there
Where noble Lazarus,
                    the Tzar, was slain,
And turns the warriors
                    over in their blood;
Should one still breathe
                    she bathes him with the water
And offers him,
                    as if in sacrament,
The dark red wine to drink,
                    the bread to eat.

At length she comes
                    to Pavel Orlovitch,
Standard-bearer
                    of his lord the Tzar,
And finds him still alive,
                    though torn and maimed:
His right hand and his
                    left leg are cut off

And his handsome chest
                is crushed and broken
So that she can see
                his lungs inside.
She moves him from
                the pool of blood
And bathes his wounds
                with clear and cool water;
She offers him,
                as if in sacrament,
The dark red wine to drink,
                the bread to eat.

When she has thus
                attended to his needs,
Pavel Orlovitch
                revives and speaks:
"Maid of Kossovo,
                my dearest sister,
What misfortune
                leads you to this plain
To turn the warriors
                over in their blood?
Who can you be
                looking for out here?
Have you lost
                a brother or a nephew?
Have you lost perhaps
                an aging father?"
And the Maid
                of Kossovo replies:
"O my brother,
                O my unknown hero!
It is not for
                someone of my blood
I'm searching:
                not an aging father;
Neither is it for
                a brother or a nephew.

136

Do you remember,
                brave and unknown warrior,
When Lazar gave
                communion to his army
With the help
                of thirty holy monks
Near the lovely
                church of Samodreza
And it took them
                twenty days to do it?
All the Serbian army
                took communion.
At the end there came
                three warrior Lords:
The first was
                captain Milosh Obilitch,
The next was
                Ivan Kossanchich,
And the last the warrior
                Milan Toplitza.
It happened that
                I stood beside the gates
As Milosh Obilitch
                passed grandly by—
There is no fairer
                warrior in this world—
He trailed his sabre
                there upon the stones
And on his head he wore
                a helmet made
Of wound white silk
                with feathers joined;
A brightly colored cloak
                hung down his back
And round his neck
                he wore a silken scarf.
As he passed he turned
                and looked at me
And offered me his
                brightly colored cloak,

Took it off and gave
            it to me, saying:
'Maiden, take this
            brightly colored cloak
By which I hope
            you will remember me—
This cloak by which
            you can recall my name:
Dear soul, I'm going
            out to risk my life
In battle for
            the great Tzar Lazarus;
Pray God, my love,
            that I return alive,
And that good fortune
            shortly shall be yours:
I will give you
            as a bride to Milan,
Milan Toplitza,
            my sworn blood-brother,
Noble Milan who
            became my brother
Before God Almighty
            and Saint John:
To him I'll give you
            as a virgin bride.'

After him rode
            Ivan Kossanchich—
There is no fairer
            warrior in this world.
He trailed his sabre
            there upon the stones
And on his head he wore
            a helmet made
Of wound white silk
            with feathers joined;
A brightly colored cloak
            hung down his back

While round his neck
                    he wore a silken scarf
And on his hand
                    he had a golden ring.
As he passed he turned
                    and looked at me
And offered me
                    the glowing golden ring,
Took it off and gave
                    it to me saying:
'Maiden, take this
                    golden wedding ring
By which I hope
                    you will remember me—
This ring by which
                    you can recall my name:
Dear soul, I'm going
                    out to risk my life
In battle for
                    the great Tzar Lazarus;
Pray God, my love,
                    that I return alive,
And that good fortune
                    shortly shall be yours:
I will give you
                    as a bride to Milan,
Milan Toplitza,
                    my sworn blood-brother,
Noble Milan who
                    became my brother
Before God almighty
                    and Saint John:
I will be the best man
                    at your wedding.'

After him rode
                    Milan Toplitza—
There is no fairer
                    warrior in this world.

He trailed his sabre
                there upon the stones
And on his head he wore
                a helmet made
Of wound white silk
                with feathers joined;
A brightly colored cloak
                hung down his back
While round his neck
                he wore a silken scarf
And on his wrist
                he had a golden torque.
As he passed he turned
                and looked at me
And offered me
                the shining golden torque,
Took it off and
                gave it to me, saying:
'Maiden, take this
                shining golden torque
By which I hope
                you will remember me—
This torque by which
                you can recall my name:
Dear soul, I'm going
                out to risk my life
In battle for
                the great Tzar Lazarus;
Pray God, my love,
                that I return alive,
And that good fortune
                shortly shall be yours
And I will take you
                for my faithful wife.'
With that the warrior Lords
                all rode away—
And so I search upon
                this field of slaughter."

Pavel Orlovitch
            then spoke and said:
"O my dearest sister,
            Maid of Kossovo!
Do you see, dear soul,
            those battle-lances
Where they're piled
            the highest over there?
That is where the blood
            of heroes flowed
In pools higher than
            the flanks of horses,
Higher even than
            the horses' saddles—
Right up to the riders'
            silken waist-bands.
Those you came to find
            have fallen there;
Go back, maiden, to your
            white-walled dwelling.
Do not stain your skirt
            and sleeves with blood."

When she has heard
            the wounded hero's words
She weeps, and tears
            flow down her pale face;
She leaves the plain
            of Kossovo and walks
To her white village
            wailing, crying out:—
"O pity, pity!
            I am cursed so utterly
That if I touched
            a greenly leafing tree
it would dry and wither,
            blighted and defiled."

translated from the Serbian with Vladeta Vucković

5
from *Batory & Lermontov*

Being, among other things, a comic lament for the decade of
the 1960s, and a private celebration, both early and late, of
the American Bicentennial and the Queen's Silver Jubilee.

for Cynouai and Laura

The Stefan Batory Poems

To begin with a name—
Katarsky—
   To begin
to leave with a name, Polish,
for a Polish ship named
for another, for Stefan Batory.
    Name of Katarsky.
Name of Stefan Batory.

To begin to leave this place
I've lived that's no more
mine than his, Katarsky's,
a village near his farm,
a land that's rich with legends
not my own, not his.

Name of Katarsky. Names
of his twins, Andrzej & Zbyszek.
Slid down haystacks with
my wife, these twins, when
she was five.
    Andrzej & Zbyszek.
Katarsky.
   After the war
when hay grew again
into haystacks, when the Poles
in England, some of them,
went home...

Katarsky, says the lady in
the shop Oh Well Katarsky sir
I'll tell you what I know
about Katarsky and that farm
and how he might as well have

145

gone on home the Russians *or*
the Germans and I
have to interrupt, say

> *no*, oh stop it now

I only wanted
a Polish name for a poem:
only wanted a way to say goodbye.

II

I wake up having dreamed of whales
To find my family sleeping in
Their berths. The breakfast menu
Is under the door: delicious
Smells in the passageway....

I can have Soki, Zupy Sniadaniowe, Jajka, Omlety, Ryby, some-
thing from the Zimny Bufet, Przetwory Owocowe on my bread,
Sery, a hot cup of Kawa bez kofeiny (coffeinevrije: decaffeinated).
Or mint tea and compôte. The day's program includes Holy Mass
in the Cinema, a matinée concert of chamber music (Vivaldi,
Handel, and Telemann), afternoon tea, an American film with
dubbed-in Polish, cocktails, bingo and dancing. Wife nor daughters
stir. I open Mickiewicz....

"Ye comrades of the Grand Dukes of Lithuania, trees of Białowieza,
Switez, Ponary, and Kuszelewo! whose shade once fell upon the
crowned heads of the dread Witenes and the great Mindowe, and
of Giedymin, when on the height of Ponary, by the huntsmen's
fire, he lay on a bear skin, listening to the song of the wise Lizdejko;
and, lulled by the sight of the Wilia and the murmur of the
Wilejko, he dreamed of the iron wolf...." What an invocation!
Comrades and trees! The trees are important.

Last night as we passed Land's End I spoke for hours with a couple
from Newcastle leaving England to emigrate to Canada. They
stared hard, saying goodbye, looking into the darkness for a last

flickering English light. They're sorry to leave but can't, so they
told me, save a sixpence in a year. I wished them luck in Canada.
And comrades. And trees.

I decide to go on deck.

III

You, Batory, an *elected* monarch.
You owed it all to Henry de Valois.
Lithuania backed the Russian Tzar,
The Church took the Archduke; the
Anti-German *szlachta* was for any
Anti-German. You from Transylvania.
But leave it to the French:
Ambassadorially, the Bishop of
Valance distributes rings to
Get the throne for edgy De Valois.
Who took one look and fled:
Brother Charles croaked
And he (Valois) was Henry Three
Sipping port in Paris.
The horsy gentry blinked and summoned—
Married you to Royal Anne Jagiellon.

How much did you know? Not as much
As Canon Koppernigk who made
His measurements at Frauenburg (which
He called Gynopolis) pretending in
His *Revolutions* that he stargazed
On the Vistula away from battlefields
And Teutonic Knights. Not as much
As Koppernigk whose system, Prince,
Because he longed for Cracow
And his youth, would run your ship
If not your ship of state aground,
But this at least: How to maintain

147

Access to the sea; how to use
A chancellor's advice. And how
With Danzig yours to drive with
Peasant infantries the Russian Bear
Beyond Livonia to the Pope.

The cavalry was not deployed—
Horses in their stables, and at hay.

IV

A day passes, the weather is rough. We meet Poles, Englishmen, Irish, Americans, Czechs, Swiss, Frenchmen, Germans, Russians, and two Japanese. Diana teaches Laura how to approach a new friend: *Was ist Ihre Name, bitte? Was ist Ihre Name?* It turns out to be Alma. Laura is delighted. Cynouai is seasick and goes early to bed. It's my night for the movies.

The Cinema is down a flight of stairs outside the dining room— and *down, low,* so very low in the ship the room should be some kind of hold or place for ballast. In the middle of *Little Big Man,* I realize with a start that I am actually under water. If we spring a leak, this theatre will instantly fill like a tank, the watertight door will be closed by a panicky steward, and there we'll be—each of us holding his nose and floating to the ceiling as Dustin Hoffman shrieks in Polish and tomahawks fall from the sky....

Was ist Ihre Name, bitte?

Was ist Ihre Name?

i

The weather improves. Serious now,
I attend to correspondence.
Here they read the news and study
Not Mickiewicz or the other unread
Poets on these shelves
But ups and downs of stocks
And the extraordinary language
Of my President reported in the
Daily Polish/English mimeo gazette.
The banalities and rhetoric of power
Dovetail with the mathematics
Of the market: Soon the brokers,
As in 1929, will sail nicely
From the upper stories
Of the highest buildings in New York,
Their sons will pluck the feathers
From their hair and look for jobs
A thousand miles from the ethnic
Bonfires of their dreams, the
Poor will stand in bread lines,
And I, a curio from 1959, will find
My clientele reduced to nuns
And priestly neophytes. I return
To Indiana—the only place
Save Utah where the Sixties,
Though Peter Michelson was waiting,
Failed to arrive.

ii

I am, as Peter thought I would be,
Going back. But slowly.
The journey takes nine days.
Unanswered letters—his and Ernie's,
Kevin's, Mrs Harris's—
They weigh on me.

My friends, my gifted student,
My daughters' much beloved nurse.

"Too much mopin' now," says P.,
"And many mumblin's...
                    But you *will*
Be coming back because although
You think yourself no gringo, John,
You are: and this is where
The gringo fighting is.
Or gringo baiting.
Or: whatever the conditions will allow.
I'll expect you here in August."

And Kevin writes: "I'm scared
Of everything and wholly lack
Direction...
                    Plus, of course,
I'm personally responsible
For all of human misery: the
Shoeless Appalachians, every
Starving Indian. And what
I like to do is eat, talk to
Charming educated people, drink
Good wine, read the best
Pornography, discuss at leisure
Every new advance
In Western decadence."

E. has written to me once a year for eight years straight. This year
it's about my poems. And his. His muse grows younger (he is over
sixty-five) as mine begins to age. My attraction to quotation,
commentary, pastiche: exhaustion? or the very method of absten-
tion that he recommends? Many days I'd be a scribe, a monk—and
I, like monk and scribe, am permitted to append the meanings that
my authors may have missed. "He abandoned himself to the
absolute sincerity of pastiche": on Ekelöf, Printz-Påhlson. Other-
wise? Poets know too much. We bring things on us. There is always
an extra place at the table: the poem, as Ernie says, arranges it....

With total serenity
He abandoned pastiche for patchouli
For patchouli and panache
He abandoned his panto-panjandrum
With utter contempt for panache
He abandoned patchouli
He abandoned himself with unspeakable simplicity
To Pastrami.

Inventions organized to dance
A variation of our lives?
Or simply evidence?
Or letters to and from our friends?
Here, the doctor said, is your scarab.
Prospero whispers in one ear
And Lenin in the other.

VI

Familiar, the dull rattle
and buzz of screws
abates; we glide....

A hundred yards away
Gothic dips and spires—
St Brendan's "floating crystal castle."

Calving from some ancient
ice sheet, pinnacles around a central
mass like sails,

it makes good time: radar brought
back only sea return—echoes from the waves.
A spotlight caught it in the fog.

Late, late...
Are we in Brendan's time?
We suffer sea return.

The ship will tilt on its keel,
roll on the last wave
over the edge of the earth.

VII

The Batory, a passenger says, once belonged to the Holland-
American line; it was, indeed, the famous "Student Ship." If this is
true, my strange sense of *déjà vu* is explained by more than the
simple fact of my being, after sixteen years, at sea again. Can it be,
in fact, that I am on the "Student Ship" once more? which flies the
colors now of Poland?

Every detail has seemed so extraordinarily familiar: the location of
rooms, the structure of the decks (did I kiss that girl from Georgia
there, just *there?*), the clever organization of space which makes
what is tight and constraining appear to be comfortable and larger
than it is. The same ship! I was on my way, eventually, to Turkey,
where I thought to save my small-town childhood love from
becoming an adult. She had spent a year in Istanbul with her
parents; her letters had grown sophisticated and knowing; I was
afraid. Seventeen and virginal, I sailed from New York thinking I
was Henry James and clutching to my heart every available illusion
about myself and the world.

Ghosting on the bridge or in the engine room, hailing Flying
Dutchmen or staring darkly at the sea, any foolish sentimental
shade aboard is mine.

VIII

Two violins, a double-bass,
Drums, piano, and trumpet—
Accordion, of course:
A curious sound.

For our tea they play us schmaltz
And polkas.

At night, the same musicians
Are transformed: they make
A fearful frantic jazz-cum-rock
With other instruments
And sing a polyphonic polyglot
Appropriate to
Mid-Atlantic revels.

On a sleeve, four gold rings of lace, an anchor above; on another,
three gold rings. I point out the captain and his second officer at an
adjacent table. Cynouai: "Then who's driving the boat?" Laura:
"It drives itself."

Over cakes, I polish my translation from the sixteenth-century
Polish of the famous Jewish Cossack, Konrad Konrad. He is not,
unlike Michelson, Matthias and Sandeen, altogether serious in his
treatment of the terrifying retribution falling upon the unfortunate
bard as a reward for the practice of his craft. Thus I render the piece
for a vanished upper-upper British accent and into an idiom which
I think would not displease, say, Edward Lear.

IX

Edgar Allan Poe
Wanted to go
To Poland.
So, probably, did Lafayette.
In 1830 he was too old.
James Fenimore Cooper
Cried: "Brothers!"
Everyone remembered Kosciuszko.
In Paris, Mickiewicz
Was eloquent: "The West,"
He said, "It dies of its doctrines!"
With Michelet and Quinet,

They cast him in bronze.
Of Lamennais: "He weeps for me."
Of Napoleon: "Come!"

Divination by Jacksonian Hickory:
Buchanan liked his ambassadorship,
His high teas with the Tzar.
In spite of Samuel Morse, that
Established Gomulka.
Churchill said: "It's no
Time for quarrels…"
Sikorsky crashed in his plane.
"Hel falls," said Hemar.
"Assassins steal our Westerplatte."

Batory, they've thrown your best
Philosopher out of Warsaw.
The one who stenographically took
The Devil's report.
I don't think Rosa Luxemburg
Would be pleased. She,
Like you, was a fighter & proud.

I like to think of Rilke's Angels
And his loving explanations to von Hulewicz.
I don't think about Esterhazy
Or Chopin. I think of Hass's poem
For his Polish friends in Buffalo.
Hass—who reads Mickiewicz
For his mushrooms.

I think of Jean Rousseau: "At least
Do not allow them to digest you!"
I think of Kazimierz Stanislaw Gzowski—
Knighted by Victoria, founder
Of the city of Toronto.
I think of Materski in the forests
Of my native Ohio: "Send no
Exiles inland." Ohio—unaware
Of 1830, of 1848.

154

Calling for my gambling debts,
The learned Purser
Quotes for me a famous
Unacknowledged source in Yiddish:
"Oh, frayg nit: 'Vus iz it?'
Los mir gehn zu machen Visit."

We approach the Gulf of St Lawrence.

X

The long aerial of Alma's German radio brings in, at last, the news. The CBC is pleased: Nixon quits. That man named Gerald Ford is president. "An honest Nixon," someone says. "A sort of Hoover type." A little late, I think, for Hoover now. But we are on the river, the sun will surely rise, and very few are interested in politics. An age of boredom dawns. New Poland steams toward Old Quebec.

I gather friends around me in
The eerie morning haze:
"'Sea hunger,'" I say, "'has gripped
The West. It will hack its way
To the Atlantic.' Friends,
I'd have rather written that
Than take the town. There died Wolfe
Victorious. 'Let us build,' said
Eisenhower, 'a canal!'

Franciscus Primus,
Dei Gratia Francorum Rex.
What, bearing such
A cross, did Cartier observe?"

Indians, I suppose. Exotic birds. Looking for Cathay, he didn't hear, his German aerial extended to its length, such twitterings as these: "I want to talk with you about what kind of line to take: I now want Kleindienst on it—It isn't a matter of trust. You have clearly understood that you will call him, give him the directions. I don't want to go off now to get us: ah! To maken ani deeeeeeeeals."

Indians. And exotic birds. At sea there is no time, and therefore do ye joke about solemnities. Therefore do ye sip Courvoisier or ponderously lie, or sleep with other people's wives. But on a river? On a waterway that Eisenhower built? *Was ist Ihre Name*, after all? Open your Mickiewicz. Abandon your panjandrum. Suffer, when the hum of screws abates, your sea return.

On one arrival here the crew abandoned ship: engineers and deck hands diving through the portholes, swimming toward the haunted isle of Parkman's Marguerite. Thevet the cosmographer at Natron heard *her* tale. Polish seamen didn't. Instead of *Little Big Man*, Warsaw played *Dziady* on a Forefather's Eve. George Sand had found it stronger stuff than *Faust*. Gomulka sent his tanks against the Czechs.

Am I guilty of obscure
Complicities, America? O Poland?
The ugly birthright of
My sinking class? Western
Nations dress themselves
To dream a dull apocalypse
While I float down that
River loved by old Champlain
And every last Algonquin
In his long canoe. I'm guilty
And in luck in lousy times.

I walk the promenade deck, look at archipelagos and tiny fishing villages, return Mickiewicz to his shelf between the propaganda and the porn. I slip my bookmark, Jessie's letter dated just about a year ago, into a jacket pocket. Then I take it out and read it once again. "These few lines," she says, "to let you hear from me. I am up but I am havin trouble with my arm an shoulder pains me like before. But I was glad to hear from you an I am glad you all are well. I thought about you all because you did say you was

Comin over before leavin an I
Didn't know what happen. I don't

Know whats wrong with people now an
I'm afraid to set out on the porch

Any more. Give my love to the girls
An write me again some time. This

Will be all for now. It's real
Cold here. Love from your friend,

Jessie Harris."

from The Mihail Lermontov Poems

DOGEARED PROEM: IN WHICH I DECIDE TO CHANGE MY NAME
BEFORE RETURNING TO ENGLAND ON A RUSSIAN SHIP AFTER
TWO YEARS OF SINCERELY TRYING TO COME TO TERMS WITH
AMERICA

Once I had a Polish friend, Zymierski.
He changed his name to Zane.
Dane Zane it became. (It's Zane Grey I blame.)
Perhaps you've seen his ivory-handled cane
In the historical museum
In Barcelona, Spain.
I resolved, in disapproval,
Never to change my name—
Even for the best of reasons,
Even in the worst of times,
Even for the sake of love, the sake of fame.

Still, today I've heard it claimed
The Baltic Shipping Company's
Investigating all the old Decembrists.
Safety first, I say.
Anyway, like Pushkin,
I'm interested in my maternal side.
(My father's fathers I cannot abide.)
No curly hair, no swarthy
Abyssinian face, I can't embrace
An Ibrahim (Great Peter's Black,
In lace); nor, like his
Successor Lermontov, find
My line extends to Ercildoune
And gnomic Thomas with his elves.
But I can reach for names
That suit me just the same.

Like old Arzeno, watchmaker
And jeweler, born in some Italian drain,
Republican and Methodist
(Rare, as the obituary read,
For one of his nativity)
Who, once he reached Ohio
"Enjoyed the largest gains
In all of Georgetown"—
And Kirkpatrick, Scottish-Irish Democratic
Miller who was Abolitionist before
The Civil War, him whose
Moniker my social-working Aunt
Still answers to
In hot unsociable and palmy
Mid-Floridian lanes.
Her Christian handle's Jean,
Not Jane.

Arzeno and Kirkpatrick! How happily
I'd hyphenate your names!
Great grandfathering immigrants
Might summon if combined
In just proportions
A Maternal Spirit
Powerful as any Abyssinian or Elf
To whom I would declaim
A strange refrain:

—"O wild Italian-Irish Lass & Muse
O take aim and snipe at
(If not slay)
The heavy and judicial German
In me called Matthias.
Protect with *sprezzatura*
And some Gaelic gall this voyager
His life
His children and his wife.
O help me put on my disguise.

Help to make me good
And wise.
I'll be to God and man
Jack Arzeno-Kirkpatrick
For an odd span
Of days
Of days and nights."

III

Ah, the stuff of greatness: Lermontov! Lermontov!
And the sources of greatness, Pushkin
And Byron. A lecture on greatness: by Olga
Our cultural commissar. An example
Of greatness, contemporary: our captain, Aram Mihailovich.
A great weight: the 20,000 tons of our ship.
A great mountain range: the Caucasus.
Great is the sauna, the caviar, the vodka
And the Volga: great is the Volga Boatman, the boatman
Himself and the song in his honor.
The bridge is great, the ballroom is great,
The bars are great (and the booze in the bars): also
The bilgewater is great and the bureaus
In the Bureaucracy: great are the drawers
Of each bureau, the pencils and papers inside,
The paper-clips and the pens.
Great is the promenade deck and the number three hatch.
Leningrad is a great city.
Moscow is a great city. The Odessa steps are
Great steps, especially in the film
By Eisenstein, the great Russian director.
A Russian passenger tells me
In the gym: "Our system is greater than yours!"
Great is the gym, the barbells and the jumping ropes:
These will make us strong! The waiter pours
Us at breakfast endless glasses
Of pineapple juice: these will make us strong.
Marx will make us strong. Lenin will make us strong.
Great & strong is the ghost of Engels
Far away in the ruins of Birmingham mills
And great is our chief engineer, Vasily Vasilyevich,
Who runs the engines turning propellers
Made by the great propeller makers of Leningrad.
Great is the Neva River and the drawbridge across it
The Winter Palace the Rostral Column the gate
Of Mihailovsky Garden the Admiralty the Palace Square
And Isaac's Cathedral, all of these sights
To be seen on a tour of the great city of Leningrad.

161

Great is cyrillic calligraphy
And beautiful too in the hands of ancient scribes
Who lived in ancient abodes before our own glorious times.
Great are our own glorious times
And great are the writers of our own glorious times
Their works and their days. Great is
The writers' union and Ivan Ivanovich its guiding spirit
And great patriotic example:
Great are his works:
Especially great are his volume of poems *Praise
To the Combine Harvester* and his novels
Bazooka and *Love in a Sewage Treatment Facility.*
Great is the port side of the ship
And the starboard, great is the fore and the aft,
Great is the bow and the bowsprit
And the Bow of Rostropovich its resin and hairs:
Great too is Shostakovich, sometimes:
His greatness appalls us in his Leningrad Symphony
If slightly less in his decadent earlier works
And his very private string quartets.
Great without doubt is the Bolshoi Ballet all the time
And great are the fountains
Of Peter the Great who was certainly great
In his time
And in his time a progressive.
Great is my cabin
Cabin 335
Where I read an anthology
Full of English and American poems
In Russian
And find in juxtaposition
One by Kenneth Koch
And one by Stephen Spender
And think continually
And think continually of what is great.

IX   A Conclusion of The Mihail Lermontov Poems
Beginning with Documentation, Paraphrase, and
Quotations Taken Down in the Revolutionary Reading
Room from a Fine Old Tome on the Thames by Allen
Wykes and Ending by Way of a Change, Once Again,
of My Name. . . .

At the other end of the river, at the other end of time, they offer
sacrifices to the Great God Lud: a bevy of virgins is flushed down
the spring at Lechlade where the River God and his friends—who
much prefer the virgins to the sheep and roosters which they
sometimes get instead, a substitution which, as we can easily
imagine, often leads to wicked floods in the Spring—run (says my
authority) *a pumping station belching out the daily fifteen hundred
million gallons of water* pouring toward us even now over the weir at
Teddington as we flow west with the tide toward Tilbury. *Hic tuus
O Tamisine Pater septemgeminus fons:* "Here, O Father Thames, is
your sevenfold fount." Among the potamologists, in fact, there is
no agreement as to exactly where it is. But Leche will do for us as it
did for Drayton in his *Polyolbion,* as it did for his friend Shipton
when he found in Trewsbury Mede that "no water floweth here-
abouts til Leche, the onlie true begetter."

If to my starboard red appear
    It is my duty to keep clear;
Act as judgement says is proper
        Port or starboard—
Back or stop her…

None of your *Wallala-leialalas* for us; that's a boatman's song with a
social function to perform. Not so long ago the captains of ships
mismanaged by members of the lively fraternity operating out of
Gravesend under the Ruler of Pilots were encouraged to dispatch
on the spot any incompetent or unlucky helmsman with appropriate
ceremonials or without. We've flown our yellow Q and blue and
orange stripes; we've blown an angry short and two long blasts on
our horn and taken on our pilot from the pilot cutter. He sings his
lonely song: *But when upon my port is seen/a steamer's starboard light
of green, /For me there's nought to do or see/that green to port keeps clear
of me.* So we are now in the hands of a specialist in rivers and can

163

hope, muttering whatever spells or mnemonics we like, to reach our proper berth with no encounters along the way with any supertankers, QE2s, ghostly Kelmscott oarsmen, estuary chains, Gordon fortifications, sunken Armadas, lightships, sands, sheers, nesses, muds, or stone outcroppings along the Hundred of Hoo. The statue of Pocahontas, who never made it home, stares at us through a Dickensian fog.

"His body doth incarnadine," remarked a jailer, "Thamesis to uncommon sanguine beauty." It was a notable execution. If Thames Head is hard to find—whether in the Mede or in the Leche or in the Pool at Seven Springs—the Thames heads are far too numerous to count. I see them vividly before me bobbing in our wake, all those lovely saints and sinners, chatting with each other about noble or ignoble deeds, drifting toward Westminster with the tide. That it should have been the *head* that always so offended! Why not, like Montezuma, pluck out hearts? No, the English god did not want hearts; you lose your head or mind in this cold country, or you hang. Your heart is yours for hoarding. Said the Virgin Queen, keeping hers to herself, red of wig and black of tooth, Tilbury protectress—"I have the heart and stomach of a king!" The pirate Drake prepared once more to burn the Spanish beard:— *with*
further protestatione that if wants
of victualles and munitione were suppliede we wold
pursue them to the furthese
that they durste
have gone....
A less official pirate, late of Scotland, said most memorably upon espying, there on execution dock, a friend: "I've lain the bitch three times and now she comes to see me hanged!" Three tides washed the bones; then he waved for days from Bugsby's Reach.... Tippling pints in Whitby's Prospect or in Ramsgate's Town we think we'd like it better in the past. When they flushed the virgins down the drain at Leche, floated heads in rivers or impaled them ornamentally on pikes—when oh they hung the pirates low beneath the tide. We'd drink we would
we'd
go pursue them durste
supply the victualles and munitione
write immortal doggerel we'd fight for Gloriana

164

Boudicca Victoria Regina choose your time
by Kitchener do your bit
for Winston spot the doodlebugs and buzzbombs
pluck out mines off Cliffe
outfox De Ruyter beat that prick Napoleon
prop on some dark night
a poor unlucky scapegoat in the new foundations my fair lady
of the bridge
and bind him there
we'd set a man to watch all night we'd do the job ourselves.
But you do not choose your time.

Lucky, guilty—
exiled or pursued,
some can choose at least a place.
As the times impinged
obscurely, George Learmont abandoned Thomas Rhymer's tower
and—as mercenary, pirate—left his home and went to organize
the cavalry in Poland for a minor Tzar. His business there was
doubtless foul. Later, Mihail Yurievich would dream of heather,
kilts and thistles, dream of George Learmont, dream of ancestors
and Malcolm and MacBeth as time—his times—impinged on him
obscurely, making him superfluous, sending him to the Dragoons
and to the mountains where he prophesied his end, with great
precision, twice. He "eloquently yearned," a learned scholar writes,
quoting his worst stuff, "to fly to high and misty crags and wake the
wild harp of Scotland once again." But the Russian god, unlike the
English, wanted hearts, great hearts—Lermontov's and Pushkin's—
a nasty bullet through each one. The Russian god would make of
both a statue and a ship—machinery converting poetry to prose,
roubles into dollars, treaties into grain, and revolution into resolu-
tions and détente. Because of which we may avoid a holocaust and
bore each other to our graves.

For my time, too, impinges oddly,
painlessly, obscurely—this kind of inbetween—
impinges surely
this time of jokes & parodies, pastiches.
An inbetween

when I don't know precisely what I want to do in time
but only where I want to go
again—
And so we're here and waiting
for a berth
to park a ship in—
waiting in a time of waiting

A time of waiting for—
For semi-retired former semi-active veteran-volunteers
of oh our still belovèd
dear and hopeful
sixties
to arise again arise
again arise
For some kind fool to build the equestrian statues
and compose the elegiac songs.

Riding high and mightily on weary white lame mare
whose forelegs beat the air
and haunches heave
his head at a tilt, his purple plumèd hat all brandishèd
on high on high
on point of keen upraisèd terrible swift sword
Squadron Leader Jack Arzeno-Kirkpatrick
sings his able arias
in honour of Air Vice-Marshal Matthias—
who has children
and a wife
who is middle class for life.

Said Marx (correctly):
men will make their history, all right,
but not exactly
as they think or choose.
(Even he had everything to lose
with that excuse.)

The signal flags unfurl and fly;
the lights flash on.

Down come blue and orange stripes,
the yellow Q:
Up go W and L, and
up goes V:
Have you got dead rats on board?
Answers ATI: *There is no cause for alarm.*
BCV replies: *Approved.*
Down come quickly *rats, no cause, approved*—
Up goes HKB:
*Hello, Komsomolka: I want
to ask you a question. Is gallantry obsolete?*
Flaps the dreaded Drake: *Think, by god,
of the Queen.* Down with HKB
and Drake, up with
M. Maksimich: *Was it the French who invented
the fashion of being bored?*
We fly the blue Pechorin: *No, it was the English.*
Taking our various oaths, we resolve
to be gallant again, and brave—
yes, Komsomolskaya—
and away with Boredom, England!
We fly *The Plundered Plowman.*
We will not plunder—
we'll plow.
We fly *The Beggared Yeoman.*
We will not beggar
we'll yodel.
*And there's a kind of waterish Tree at Wapping
whereat sea-thieves
or pirates are catched napping.*

Oh, our resolutions are serious enough
in spite of the jokes
and in spite of our preoccupations
—the baggage, the passports—
and we really do propose to lead a better life this year
than last
though we do not tell ourselves exactly how.

Standing on the promenade
in attitudes
of suspicion, attention, or anticipation
hoping for some fine
benign surprise
each of us looks at the land
thinking still of the sea.
Each contrives
to be abstracted one last time in sea-thoughts
or in dreams
before the symbolical stranger
posing as a customs agent
or a clerk or porter in a small hotel or pension
asks the question symbolical strangers ask
which only actions answer

and each, I think, hums a variation
on the final chorus
of the tune
—changing names and faces,
touching all the graces—
that he's whistled up and down the decks
through afternoon & afternoon.

—*O wild Italian-Irish Lass & Muse*
protect with sprezzatura
and some Gaelic gall this voyager
his life
his children and his wife.
O help me take off my disguise.
Help to make me good
and wise.
I've been to God and man
Jack Arzeno-Kirkpatrick
for an odd span
of days
of days and nights.

6
New Poems

My Youngest Daughter: Running Toward an English Village Church

Sunday, then. In Trumpington. And nearby bells.
My daughter runs among the village graves
this foggy January morning of her early youth
as I lie late in bed
and watch her from my window.

I know she holds her breath.
Superstitious, she'll hold it till she passes by
the final marker near the door & disappears inside.
If you breathe in cemeteries
you inhale evil spirits!
What do you inhale when you breathe in stony
churches or in bedrooms where you wake alone
and realize you cannot tell
your child's superstition from her faith?

Beyond the church, a village green, a meadow,
the pleasures and the picnics
of next spring. I tell her
not to hold her breath in graveyards.
Watching her red coat become a gaudy blur
against the brilliant hoarfrost,
I realize I'm holding mine.

At a Screening of Gance's *Napoleon*: Arts Theatre, Cambridge

In the shadow of the eastern towers of Kings
and in the Sunday-dinner darkened theater where
Lydia Keynes once danced the frozen breath away
from puffing Cambridge dons, we eat our

sandwiches between parts three and four of
Abel Gance's reconstructed, spliced-together,
silent, five-hour epic on Napoleon.
I am, said Bonaparte, *a rock thrown into space.*

We can believe it. Spinning giddily from images
of Corsica to images of storms tossed up by
the Sirocco, the Convention, and Rouget de Lisle,
we'd clutch at almost anything, even this

unfashioned rock that tumbles through the space
of an unfinished film and cries: *to make
yourself well understood, speak to people's eyes!*
Our eyes are red; we rub them in the interval

and stuff our mouths with cheese & chutney, wash
it down with beaujolais kept cool in a thermos.
Somewhere in part two, reel seventeen or so,
beneath the guns of Admiral Hood pounding batteries

outside Toulon where Dugommier attacks the captured
port, Bonaparte assumed command. The silence
of all that exhausted us: this black & white morality
keeps its moral to itself or hasn't got one yet.

Shall we see in Antonin Artaud's Marat, or even
in Maxudian's Barras, the cruel stuff of History?
or do we gape at mysteries of Art? (We might have
left before the Terror if we hadn't brought our

sandwiches and wine.) Abel Gance maintained that
he had made Prometheus. He said (aloud)
he'd found a cinematic style capable of Vision.
Then the markets crashed and Jolson's busy progeny

made all those early talkies sing & pay their way.
War's anachronism, said this hero of the triple screen,
tearing every city down in sight. And Gance:
All those polyvision sequences to come, you've seen.

Ahhhh! we said, watching Cinerama in the fifties,
waiting for the famous rollercoaster ride that actually
made kids throw up their popcorn. These final reels
will march us out beyond the foothills through the Alps,

the screen split into three to make us gasp:
as triptych or as trinity, *Les Mendiants de la Gloire*
will traipse behind Napoleon into Italy—
we'll never see the Empire or a sunset by the Loire.

We'll wait, like Josephine, with spots before our eyes:
those blinking phantoms a machine's already loosed,
the gangling ghosts of Robespierre, Marat,
the feminine, impassioned, & most elegant Saint-Just.

Unpleasant Letter

i

Information has this day been laid
By R.L. Waters

Of the Cambridgeshire Constabulary
Who states that you—

That *you* on 28.4.77
Did at Sidgwick Avenue in the said

City during the hours of darkness
Cause a pedal cycle

To be on the road when it did not
Carry (a) one bright lamp which showed

White light to the front
And (b) one bright lamp which showed

Red light to the rear
Visible from a reasonable distance

Contrary to Section 74
Of the Road Traffic Act, 1972. You

Are summoned to appear on 23.5.77
At the hour of 10:00 a.m.

Before the Magistrates' Court sitting
At the Court House, Guildhall,

To answer the said
Information and statement of facts.

ii

No white light to the front? No red
Light to the rear? O

Constable Waters, O pedal cycles
O ancient magistrates and ancient guilds

Of Cambridge: O reason & reasonable distance
O information that's laid

O hours of deepest darkness O lights
Both white & red which flash

Toward the future and signal
The past & the passing: O vision O visions

I was illuminated all over all tingling
Fluorescent & flashing in

Every direction at once: I had read
For a day in your citadels Marlowe O Newton

O John Maynard Keynes
And I've fled to the silts & peats & clays

Of the Fens and dug in
And dug into the prehistorical Fens

Where I wait for you
With my hoard of knowledge and flints

With my bicycle chain and both of my pedals
With my deer's antler and medals

Where I wait with my middle-American vowels
Where I summon you all

To the Stone-age shaft where I hide & abide
With the ghosts

Of hairy Fenmen: Constable, magistrate, prefect,
Bursar, provost, torturer, cook—

With a bright white light to the front: with
A bright red light to the rear—

I summon you all: all of you: to appear!

E. P. in Crawfordsville

*for D. D. in South Bend lecturing on
"Enlightenment and Christian Dissent"*

He was *en provence* for sure
at Wabash college—
Writing there to Mary Moore
of Trenton, "Grey eyes..."

Writing *Cino*: "Bah! I have
sung women in three
cities...", putting up an
unemployed actress,

getting fired, *Gay Cino
of quick laughter,
Cino, of the dare, the jibe.*
What, asked Possum more

than once, does Ezra Pound
believe? In light. In
light from the beginning,
in gardens of the sun—

But "'Pollo Phoibee, old
tin pan", in Crawfordsville?
Age des lumières! Bold
Polnesi, Jefferson, Voltaire—

light inside the acorn-seed
on Zeus's aegis-day
when he'd become indeed
the lack-land Cino

having sung & sung the sun
for thirty years in
every kind of city, light
converging into one

great ball of crystal
silent as some Hoosier
Presbyterian at prayer
along the Wabash.

F. M. F. from Olivet

(remembering Joseph Brewer)

Hueffer's Trade Route
didn't really pass
through Olivet, but Ford
had written anyway

to Italy: *Dear Bertran
de Struwwelpeter
y Bergerac*—remembering
the other's *Deah*

*ole Freiherr von
Bluggerwitzkoff, lately
Baron of the Sunken
Ports, etcetera*—

explaining that
a Small Producer might,
just there in Olivet, though
it was not Provence,

produce: "If it's good
enough for me it's
good enough for you,
concealed son o'

the authoress of *John
Halifax Gentleman*
though you be." His cor-
respondent queried him

re Distribution: of ideas,
of light, through a
Trade Route called
a Lino or a Monotype....

For investment, there
was no return: Bertran of
Rapallo from Cathay
to Bluggerwitzkoff, ripe

as Memphis cotton picked
and sorted to a pip &
woven into double-breasted
stripes in Michigan:

"Does Olivet USE my text
books? Will the clog-
dancer ANSWER a few civil
questions? Let me put

it in another form: I
do not want YOUR job,
I do not want the
JOB that you have got."

Words for Sir Thomas Browne

i

If melancholy is a sadness with no reasonable cause,
your son Tom's death at sea produced in you a grief

and not a melancholy. You would define, define again,
whose testimony helped convict, in 1655,

two witches in the court of Matthew Hale. Gentle man,
they hung on Suffolk gallows till they died.

You bore no kind of malice towards them, either one,
and you studied to avoid all controversy always.

But if no witches did the Devil's work, it followed
that no works were done among us by the Spirits,

and from that, no doubt "obliquely", that the hierarchy
of creation would collapse & neither New Philosophy

nor love could save the soul of your young Tom
who read & praised the pagans on his ship *whose noble*

straynes, you thought, *may well affect a generous mind.*
Amazed at *those audacities, which durst be nothing,*

and return into their Chaos once again, you recommended
orthodoxy and you testified for Matthew Hale.

ii

Death was occupation and preoccupation both in Norwich
where you practiced medicine, exploded vulgar errors,

contemplated cinerary urns. You did not *secretly implore*
& wish for plagues, rejoyce at famines, or *revolve*

ephemerides in expectation of malignant aspects & eclipses
like certain others of your trade. Your prayers

went with the husbandmans, desiring *everything in proper*
season, that neither men nor times be out of temper.

But they were deeply & profoundly out of temper, the men
and times in your extraordinary time. New Science

studied to discern the cause and was itself part cause
and part effect. Love got on with its peculiar,

frail, sublunary affairs: and though you'd be *content that*
we might procreate like trees without conjunction,

husbands awkwardly attended to their husbandry, and you
yourself begot a dozen saplings. Of the seven who survived,

Edward was the firstborn and the doctor, but Tom was your
particular delight—& like to make, you thought, at once

a navigator & a scholar on that ship of Captain Brookes—
and like to take the draughts of all things strange.

iii

Pythagoras and Lucan, Epicurus too: he took the draughts
of these and dwelt on noble suicides, on transmigrations,

and on souls that dwelt in circuits of the moon or souls
eternally annihilated in eternal night.

Audacious draughts: they'd make a generous mind so drunk
it might conceive itself invaded by the speech of Vulteius

and urge, in some engagement where a Netherlandish Pompey
stole the victory & then prevented honorable escape,

the sober Roman medicine you feared. How did Thomas die?
If he fell upon his sword, or, lost to Admiral Kempthorne,

lit a powder keg and blew his ship to kingdom come,
we never heard. If some malefic doctor set about to loose

a plague, or grinning crones beside a rocky coast at dawn
spun almanacks and made a storm, you never said.

You did your work: you sought to cure the ill & comforted
the dying, you strangled mice and chickens on your

kitchen scales to see if *weight increaseth when the vital
spirits flee*, you demonstrated that the elephant

indeed has joints, that beavers do not ever *in extremity
bite off their stones*, that no bear brings her

young into the world *informus and unshapen* to fashion them
by licking with her tongue, that Eve & Adam had no navels

and that Jesus wore (a Nazerite by birth) short hair.
Often you returned to your initial, fundamental ground:

Whatever impulse be unlocked by Lucan's strains, whatever
operation be insinuated in us when, Satanic,

we're inhabited by arguments which say *necessity* or *chance*
or *fate*, a lucid sense of order could, you thought,

when mixed in some alembic with humility & grace, explain
and purge away (though witches must, alas, be hanged).

iv

As *though the soul of one man passed into another,*
opinions, after certain revolutions, do find men & minds

like those that first begat them.

                              Staring fixedly at Tom's
last letter in your hand, thinking of that trial where

one alleged his chimney had been cursed & yet another that
his cart had been bewitched and also all his geese,

you well might suddenly embrace that sweet & generous heresy
that tempted you when you were young: that all are saved—

yourself & Tom, those witches in the court of Matthew Hale,
Epicurus, Lucan & Pythagoras, cruel doctors who revolve

ephemerides, husbands who attend to husbandry, sons and
daughters, brothers aunts & sisters, wives.

And yet you said: *God saves whom he will...*
and thought the wretched women damned at Edmund's bury.

And thought you heard Tom's ship explode at sea.

Words for Karl Wallenda

[*Wallenda was the great aerialist, killed in a fall in San Juan in 1978.
His most famous stunt, in one performance of which several members
of his acrobatic family were killed or injured, was called 'The Pyramid.'*]

i

& is
the rope

as narrow as
these

lines
& would

you walk it
get

a family
on it

build
your house

upon it
Karl Wallenda

not of stone
but of

their bones
& yours

agility &
will

and would
you cut

your losses
& your net

& catch the
less compulsive

when they
stumble

tumble
past you

in your arms
or watch

them fall?

& would
you call

your house
a pyramid

& you
the Cheops

in it
& the priest

& mason
of it too

who know
or knew the

reasons &
the seasons

the rivers
& the winds

& is
your house

as narrow as
these

lines
& would you

try to
move it on

a rope
as narrow

as these
lines

until it
falls

around you
to the

clownish
circus floor

laws of balance
all intact

but in-laws
tackless

sailing by
& fall-

ing
past you

Karl Wallenda
on all

sides

ii

& would you
leave

that fallen
house

to walk alone
one morning

in San Juan
& did you

take an easy
walk this

morning in
San Juan

& did you
lean

185

into the
sea breeze

with a smile
until it

stiffened for
a passage

to the
chambers of

a pyramid
that no

one saw
or had foreseen

& did you lean
Wallenda

toward it
& then

fall
& did you

fall like
Icarus

or Troy
did you fall

like Adam
did you lean

all human
out of balance

did you fall
& did you

fail to rise
upon the wind

or walk
upon the water

did you fall
& did you

slide into
the passage

in the
northern face

& pass into
the chamber

for the King
& did you

leave us
in amazement

& on ropes
as narrow

as these
lines

& with
your name

upon your lips
Wallenda

Rostropovich at Aldeburgh

I   As Soloist

The Haydn Concerto in C with Britten's cadenzas:
He flies through these (the cadenzas)
Like an Aeroflot plane, like a Concordsky,
Out of the eighteenth century into our own
And then back.
It's difficult for us to tell
Which of these ages he's happiest in
Or with which composer:
Or whether if all of us wore our wigs
And our wings
To tea at the Maltings
We'd feel completely out of our time
Or merely well dressed.

II   As Conductor

The Shostakovich 14th.
Which broods on
Death and is eloquent.

His wife, Galina Vishnevskaya,
Sings with Ulrik Cold
The texts by Apollinaire, Lorca,

Kuchelbecker, and Rilke.
Which brood on
Death and are eloquent.

The widow of the composer
Sits in the audience.
What we applaud for is what

In each of us might, if we're lucky,
Survive. And he applauds back at us,
Being Russian. He's beaming and

Bouncing, blessing us all with his smile.
He kisses the hand of his wife,
The cheek of the first violinist,

The balding head of every balding
Percussionist:
One, two, three, and four.

A Wind in Roussillon

I

The Tramontane that's blowing pages
of an unbound book through Roussillon
departs on schedules
of its own....

Et nous, les os... et nous, les os.
And us, the bones.

II

The train departs from Austerlitz on time.
After Carcassonne, Tuchan,
wheat and barley dry up in the sun
& trees appear hung heavily
with cherries, lemons, oranges.

Red tiled roofs are angled oddly
on the little houses in the hills below Cerdagne.
Gray slate's left behind.

By the tracks
a villager has nailed up a goat's foot
and a sunflower to the door
that opens on his vineyard
circled by a wall of heavy stones.

III

In French, the words of Mme T. about les îles Malouines sound
nearly as bizarre as ads for the religious kitsch at Lourdes translated
into English in the same edition of *Le Monde*... "A see-through
plastic model of the Virgin with unscrewable gold crown enables
you to fill the image up with holy water from a tap." And Mme T.,
qui a félicitée les forces armées, swells in French to the dimensions of
a Bonaparte: *les plus merveilleuses du monde... le courage et l'habileté
ont donné une nouvelle fierté à ce pays et nous ont fait comprendre que
nous étions vraiment une seule famille.*

Et nous, les os: vraiment une seule famille.

IV

Low hills dense with yellow broom!
Cactus, thistles, wild mountain roses;
lavender and holly and convolvulus.
Above the rows of plane trees,
olive groves root down through rock.
Above the olive groves, cypresses & pines.

Down the valley under Canigou
a helicopter dips and passes overhead,
circles the Clinique Saint-Pierre
whining like a homing wasp.
Landing in an asphalt parking lot,
it scatters old men playing skittles, boules.
Young men wearing orange flight suits
carry something human
wrapped in white inside.

V

The name of one low, ruined house
in Perpignan is John
and Jeanne. (It's in another country.)
When great winds pass the threshold
nothing sings or appears.

It's John & Jeanne
and from their graying faces
falls the plaster of day. (Far off
the most ancient one,
the arch daughter of shadows.)

You build a fire in the cold great hall
and you withdraw.
(Your name is Yves Bonnefoy.)
You build it there, and you withdraw.

VI

My hostess came to Perpignan from Dublin more than forty years
ago. Now in her late sixties, she lives in the third floor flat of an
elegant eighteenth-century house in what were once the servants'
quarters. The walls are full of books on Cathar heresies and
Albigensians and Templars. When the south of France was flayed
for twenty years in the Crusades, blood ran all the way from
Montségur to the Queribus Château before it finally dried. Mme
Danjou came here with the Quakers when the Spanish Civil War
broke out and helped Republican refugees across the border at Port
Bou. Four years later she was helping Jews across the border in the
opposite direction when the Roussillon was occupied by the Nazis.
Denounced by a neighbor, she was thrown in jail where she waited
for the train that would take her to a prison camp in Germany. Like
other European women of her generation, she is tough. "One felt,"
she says, struggling for a moment with the English that she rarely
speaks these days, "that one had work to do." The war had ended
by the time the Nazis sent the train.

VII

Not only the delimited circumferences
but also all the white stone houses
in the streets of southern Catholic cemeteries
speak of walled towns by Vauban
or by his foretypes in the Middle Ages or before.
This silent town within the town of Collioure
where Derain and Picasso paid their bills
with paintings no one wanted yet
fortifies itself against the naked bathers
and the tourists at the Templiers.
I intrude upon the silent tenants searching
for Antonio Machado.

The wealthy dead inhabit their expensive homes
and wait impatiently for quick descendants
to arrive and fill each empty room marked *reservée*.
The poor lie down in dresser drawers stacked high
in marble walls around a central Calvary
and whisper without any *nouvelle fierté à ce pays*:
"Nous étions vraiment une seule famille."

Machado fled from Franco's armies
first to Barcelona, then across the border
with some refugees. Dying, he came
on foot, and in the rain, and with his mother.
He left the room they gave him only once
to walk alone along the streets of Collioure
before they brought him here.
He sings these dead his mortal words forever.
Globo del fuego... disco morado...

The sun that parched the bones
dries up the town, dries up the southern sea.
Savilla is distant and alone.
Sol. Soleil.
Castile, and Collioure! Machado.

VIII

With knife or nail or glass someone clumsily
has scratched into the blackened wooden gate
that's chained high up beyond one's reach
at Fort Saint-Elme: *Privée, Bien Gardée.*

A small green lizard darts between two stones.
It looks to be deserted in the tower, and yet
it's difficult to tell. Everything inside
has been restored. They say it's lived in now.

Climbing here, I heard two cuckoos answering
each other down the valley. A kestrel hovers high
and drops to earth the far side of the tower.
No sound now but northern wind on fortified étoile.

The level sea below me mirrors Le Château Royal
that Dugommier won back for revolution after
Dufour's treason turned the cannon of Saint-Elme
on quiet Collioure for money and for Spain.

From the col de Banyuls through Port-Vendres
they'd advanced. Then, bien gardée, Saint-Elme.
A captain stood about where I stand, bargaining.
Dufour let him quickly through the gates.

No one sang the cruel cannonade they loosed
on the Château which burned away the Middle Age
from rampart, hall and tower. Dugommier won back
the smoking bones before which once some

pitiful last troubadour sang out to Templars
gazing down at him beside the sea. No one gazes
down from Fort Saint-Elme. Nor do I sing out
Dòna, maries de caritat...
                              Lady, mother of charity...
I was born too late....

IX

Tour de la Massane, Tour de Madeloc. Towers like these stretch along the backbone of the Pyrenees and look down on the plain of Roussillon, the southern coast, and Spain. By day the little garrisons would signal to each other with a puff of smoke, by night with fire. Valerius Flaccus, Commandant at Madeloc, left his chiselled mark on the great rock. In Rome, they put him on a coin. In Roussillon, les os. *Que malvaise chançon de nos chanté ne seit*, he might have said a little later and a little to the west. What he said, in fact, was this:

VALERIUS FLACCUS
PRAEFECTUS PRAESIDII MONUMENTUM JUSSIT
VIVUS SIBI CONDI LOCO
INTERCEPTO ET EMUNITO

The buried temple spits no mud or rubies out. The sun pours down upon the tower that now relays the television news from Paris, London, Rome, and even as far off as Las Malvinas or The Lebanon. I sit in my hotel and drink in martial music from the streets of Buenos Aires. Then we see Israeli tanks annihilate Beirut. Communication is a subtle thing through our electric sepulchre. In the Punic wars, Valerius could only talk in hyperbolic terms with smoke and fire.... Power hymns instalments to its spirit now in all works of impatience: wars, towers, rituals, TV. In memory, Valerius, you arise. Like an occult language found in an iron-bound book.

X

Mother of charity, Mother of consolation,
Your house is not La Tour Madeloc,
Mother of bones, Mother of dissolution.

Lady of leisure, Lady of Roussillon,
Maître Xinxet has blackened your hermitage,
Lady of landfall, Lady of languors.

Mother of ostentation, Mother of ordure,
Neptune rests in your chapel,
Mother of noon, Mother of nightshade.

Lady of purdah, Lady of purchase,
The village cries out for rain,
Lady of drought, Lady of departures.

Mother of Jesus, Mother of jackals,
The pilgrim is flaying the Jew,
Mother of olives, Mother of obeisance,

Lady binding the book in leather & iron,
Mother of scattered pages,
Work of secret patience, Tramontane.

Northern Summer

The flight of sentimentality through empty space.
Through its elliptical hole
an heraldic blackbird's
black wings, yellow beak, round eyes, with the yellow
ring, which defines its inner empty
space

—Göran Sonnevi

I The Castle

                  Occupies
a picturesque
commanding strong position
on the summit of a cliff some forty
feet in height
the base of which is covered
up at flood tide by the waters of the Forth.
Large, magnificent, commodious
with rock nearby and wood and water to afford
the eye a picture of a rare
and charming beauty
forming a delightful and romantic spot
the sight of which
could not but amply compensate et
cetera
                  the language of a tour book
threading aimlessly
through sentimental empty space.

Or build on, say, an Edward's language
to his dear and faithful cousin
Eymar de Valance
like a second generation builds upon
the ruins of a first?

                  finding not
in our
Sir Michael Wemyss

196

good word
nor yet good service and
that he now shows himself in such a wise
that we must hold him traitor
and our enemy we do command you that ye
cause his manor where we lay
and all his other manors to be burned his lands
and goods to be destroyed
his gardens to be stripped all bare
that nothing may remain
and all
may thus take warning—

Language
moving upon consequence
Consequence
upon a language: Flight
of an heraldic bird
through space that is inhabited.

Some say Bruce had raised his standard here.

I live between the castle and the coal mine
in a folly. It's the truth.
They put a roof on it last year. I have
a room, a window on the sea.

                    Strange to say, I
haven't seen my host yet,
Captain Wemyss.
He's holed up in his castle in this awful rain.
I'm holed up in my folly with
my pads and pens.
If the sun comes out this month, maybe yet
we'll meet
a-walking in the garden O.

                    "Baron Wemyss of Wemyss"
all the old books call
his many forbears.
Do I just shout out *hello there
Wemyss of Wemyss?*
Seven centuries of purest Scottish pedigrees,
says Mr F., the Edinburgh historian.
Twenty-seven generations.
I can offer
just one eighth of watery Kirkpatrick.

The flight of sentimentality through empty space!
A rhetoric, at least; (an awkward line).
The flight of Sentiment
is through a space that's occupied.

This space is occupied, all right,
and I am guest
of both the present and the past.

                    The past
begins in caves,
the Gaelic *Uamh* soon enough becoming Wemyss.

James the Fifth surprised
a band of gipsies in one cave, drinking there
and making merry. Though he
could join them incognito in his famous role
as Godeman of Ballangeich
and share their mad hilarity, James the Sixth
would only shout out *treason*
when he panicked of a sudden, claustrophobic,
in a *Uamh* become a mine.

Above the caves and mines they built this house.

And put a chaplain in it! I find there was
no piper here, and worse, no bard—
But Andrew Wyntoun, a prior of St Serf,
wrote a family chronicle in verse
& praised
              An honest knycht
and of good fame
Schir Jhone of Wemyss by his rycht name.

Well, if I'm the guest of absent hosts
the cost of lodging here a while
is neither waived
nor anywhere within my calculation—
(the flight of Sentiment
is not
through empty space)

Did Mynyddog Mynfawr, camped along the Forth,
feed the brave Gododdin mead and wine
a year
a year
a year?

Or did he send them sober down his mine?

III THE MINE

The flight through empty space of Sentiment
—mentality! There's nothing
sentimental
within sight of this abandoned mine.
From where I stand
I'd talk about dead gods, I think.
                    From where I stand on this
deserted beach
between the castle and the mine
I think I'd say the legates
of the dead god Coal
had built his image here to look
exactly like a gallows made of iron & alloy
high enough
to hang a giant from—

The tower's erect upon the hill, but nothing moves.

Who worked here once?
No Free Miners from the Forest of Dean
have hewn the coalface down the ages
here at Wemyss from when
the coughing grey-eyed servants
won the coal
for monks at prayer in freezing Dunfermline
but virtual slaves. No *gales*, no lease
for them.
            "Coal beneath the soil
shall be inherited with soil
and property." The lairds of Fife could pack
a Privy Council and by act of law
reduce a man to serfdom. He
was bought or sold
along with his equipment. His child
went underground at six
to earn an extra seven pence
lest he sail to Noroway with Sir Patrick Spence.

The tower's erect upon the hill, and nothing moves.

When fire leapt down the tunnel, forked and dove,
an age had come and gone. The
nation voted Labour
but the coal board blundered here in Wemyss
at once.
            The lift plunged down
through all that soaring iron and alloy, down
to where the caves and tunnels
smoulder uselessly and spread the fire
on inland through
bituminous rich veins. It could burn
a hundred years. It could burn as far as London.

Miles of heavy cable lie around me
on the beach. Almost ankle-thick, it unravels
like a length of rope left over
from a hanging. It raised and lowered the lift.
The lift descended with amazing speed.
With amazing speed
the fire leapt down the tunnel, forked and dove.
Everyone, I think, got out.

A tanker steams across the bleak horizon.

The tower's erect upon the hill.

IV   A Queen

John Knox said the visit of the Queen
had raised the price
of wild fowl sufficiently
that partridges were sold at half a crown.
He was not a sentimental man.
Of the Regent's coronation
he'd remarked: "Seemly
as to put a saddle on the back
of an unruly cow."
                              O belle
et plus que belle crooned
Mary's friend, Ronsard. Better him than Knox
for gentle conversation?
Better all the Medicis & better maybe
little sick king Frank
whose inflammation of the middle ear
and abscess of the brain
were dear to Calvin.
                              And yet her keen eyes
danced out of a window here
in February, 1565.
It was cold that year in Fife.
Every fireplace here at Wemyss was blazing
full of fine Wemyss coal
when Mary gazed at Charles Darnley riding by.
Yesterday was warm & bright
when Peggy, who's the cook, pointed
out the window, showing me
where Darnley had dismounted. I had come
to get a pan to heat some water in.
He had come to woo a queen,
win the Matrimonial Crown and full equality
of Royal right, make every kind
of mischief in the realm. The empty space
between the window and
the place he stood beside his horse
in sexy tight black hose was filled at once
with Feeling—

202

Darnley sang a song more serious than Ronsard's
and Bothwell entered in his
little book that Kirk o'Field's convalescent
suffered from *roinole* and not
petite verole—
           syphilis, not smallpox.
But that was later on.
At Wemyss it was a sentimental morning.

V   A PRINCE

Or talk about Charles Edward then.
Charles, Edward, Louis,
Sylvester, Maria, Casimir, Stewart.
The Bonnie Prince himself,
the grand Chevalier. To the Forty-Five
this castle sent Lord Elcho.
Kindred of my own kin's forbears, my
brooding and attainted
absent host,
           he gazed from Holyrood
through gilded ballrooms & out casement windows
at the gillies & the pipers & the clans
weighing odds, meditating
languages—Gaelic, French, the
lisped Italian English of his Regent Prince.

     The King enjoy his ain again?
Doubtful, but for honour
one must risk in any case this autumn theatre
although it issue
in a winter's desolation....

Claymore!—
        (or is it *Gardyloo?*)—echoes
even now from Holyrood
through Fife. Beneath those Strathspey
dancers' feet when Elcho's mother

led off celebrations
of the rout at Prestonpans,
history smouldered with surprises
older than the coal fields
on the Wemyss estate.
Language moved upon inconsequence
and consequence
at once: *Will you see me*
to my quarters? and
                    No quarter...

as if you'd hear two voices whispering
behind you while you stared
down Royal Mile thinking of the sheltered hollow
under Arthur's seat....

The empty space between the window
framing Elcho and the place the clansmen camped
filled up in time with sentimental tales
and the progeny
of all those partridges
whose price the visit of the Scottish Queen
had raised, said Knox, to half a crown.
And yet his line of vision then
was tangent to
the flight of an heraldic bird
whose spiral into time
was on a furious northern wind—
vehement,
and with a terrifying sound.

VI   A VOICE

I hear my mother's voice reading Stevenson—
or is it Scott? Someone's wandering lost
among the heather. I must be eight or nine.
I know I should be reading this myself,
but when I read the words the voice I hear
ceases to be hers....
                              There is a space
I have not learned to fill
somewhere between printed marks and sounds
and I am lost in some way too
among the heather, frightened of the distances
when all I want to do is drift on lang
uage into dream....
                              "Cha n'eil Beurl' agam..."
someone says, but I follow him
in any case on hands & knees in terror.
Have I got the silver button in my teeth?
Am I papered for the murder of that
Campbell back in Appin? We're through
the cleft, the Heugh of Corrynakiegh,
and now the moor: it's black and burned
by heath fires. Moorfowl cry.
The deer run silently away from us....

Or am I underneath the castle of my enemy?
And is my enemy my only friend? I hear
the sentinel calling out in English
All's well, All's well
but we crawl off toward a hovel
made of stone & turf & thatch. There's
a fire inside, and over it a small iron pot.
The ancient crone who's stirring it
offers me a boiled hand
                              to steal away
some gentleman's attention
from his Ovid... and pack him off to bed
with images to mingle
with his dreams, said R.L.S. to Baxter.

205

And Scott: that "laws & manners
cast a necessary colouring;
but the bearings, to use heraldic language,
will remain the same,
though the tincture may be different
or opposed...."
                    Bearings... tincture...
Theft and Dream,
flight of an heraldic bird through language,
and my mother's voice.

Who are the Kirkpatricks? where is Abbotsford?
How can poor sick R.L.S., listening with
his Hoosier wife, hear off in Samoa "beaten bells"
from just across the Firth?

For a moment, laws and manners seem no
more than colouring. Charles Edward back in Paris
casts a medal of himself—*Carolus Walliae
Princeps*—and the future hangs
on messages delivered by the likes of
Alan Breck from men like Cluny
in his cage—
language moving upon consequence....

                    But time has gone to live with
Waverleys and Balfours, with townies
like Rankeillor and his lowland lawyer ilk.
I am awake in Fife. I hear
the distant echoes of my mother's voice reading.
Sentiment's transfigured into history,
and history to sentiment.

206

VII KIRKCALDY

In Kirkcaldy one considers economics.
We need a dozen eggs. I leave my folly, catch
a bus near Wemyss, and walk around
this "old lang toun" that bears the name
of Mary's last defender.
Loyal old Kirkcaldy, last
support and stay of an unlucky queen,
scourge of Bothwell, keeper
of the craggy rock in Edinburgh
out of which your one-time friend John Knox
would pry you even with his
final fetid breath—
                                   Linoleum?
In June
descendents of those Covenanters Cromwell shot
treat their jute with linseed oil
where William Adam, stone & lime Vanbrughian,
built in Gladney House
a Netherlandish lesson for his sons
and Adam Smith returned in early middle age
and wrote.

Did Elcho see young Robert Adam on the castle wall
where John Knox saw Kirkcaldy? each one
moving through the crystal chambers
of his mind to build more perfect measurements
before the cannon fired
of distances heraldic birds might fly,
language moving upon consequence
to say *Nobility*,
Salvation, Space?
                          When Adam left
Kirkcaldy grammar school
for Edinburgh, Smith enrolled at
Glasgow, never mentioning (when he
returned at forty-five) the Forty-Five.
"The workmen carry nails instead
of money to the baker's shop and alehouse.

The seat of empire should remove itself
to that part of the whole
contributing the greatest share to its support.
In sea-port towns a little grocer
can make forty-five percent upon a stock. Capitals
increased by parsimony
are diminished by misconduct, prodigality...."
And not a word about the bonded miners
in the collieries & salt pits.

Economies! Those workmen died
in nailers' dargs to earn a casual footnote.
That parsimony made a bigot certain he was saved,
his neighbour rightly damned.
That seat of empire never moved;
its rebel colonies themselves became imperious.
Those country houses made by Adam and his sons
rose up with fortresses
they built at Inverness on orders straight
from Cumberland, which bled.

The smell of jute on linseed
stinks of deprivation: linoleum peels off floors
of little grocers in this town
where faces in the baker's shop and alehouse
thirst for darker oils
sucked up Shell, BP, and Exxon rigs
from underneath the bottom of the sea.

The Regent dragged Kirkcaldy from his rock
and hung him on the gallows Knox prepared him for:
face against the sun.
His blinded eyes beheld a crazy German
sitting firmly on a Stuart throne.
History gave William Pitt *The Wealth of Nations*,
the brothers Adam peel-towers & Fort George.

Beggared sentiment flew straight into the hills

And metamorphosed there in Ossianic melancholy.
James Macpherson heard, he said,
the howling of a northern wind; he heard old men
chanting through the night about the woods
of Morven; Selma filled, he wrote,
with names & deeds—Fingal's, Oscar's, Gaul's—
but language threaded aimlessly through empty spaces
& through languorous dreams, *with rock nearby
and wood and water to afford the eye
a rare and charming beauty, the sight of which
could not but amply compensate*
admirers of the sentimental and the picturesque.
Where better read a "forgery" than in a folly?

And shall I like these poems
that David Hume defended when he found
the heroes' names authenticated
by an inventory of all the Highland mastiffs?
Napoleon did, who never heard of Dr Johnson,
but who carried *Fingal* into battle
imitating, now and then, with relish,
the Ossianic style in his memos & dispatches.
And Goethe, caught up in the turmoil
of his *Sturm und Drang*, built
the European Zeitgeist from a massive
mountain sadness caught in far Temora.
Staring at Macpherson's book,
they filled the emptiness before their eyes
with what they were.
                              It was an age
of forgeries & fakes: Pretenders
old and young, gothic ruins in the garden,
memories of casket letters, padded
coats and powdered wigs. And while Macpherson
roamed the hills in search of Gaelic bards,
a London dealer named Buchanan
sold the Earl of Wemyss a phony Venus

signed *Van Dyck*: "the sight of which could
not but amply compensate", etcetera,
Buchanan whispered softly in the noble ear,
and rubbed his hands, and grinned.
Staring at the canvas on his castle wall,
the Earl filled the emptiness before his eyes
with what he thought he saw.

"The Erse Nation may be furious with Lord North,
for even Fingal tells him so,
but adds: 'And yet, my Lord, *I* do not
desert you.'" Walpole, 1782.
Macpherson travelled south & changed his style,
learning, it appears, a language moving
upon consequence, and consequently moved among
the circles of the powerful & into spaces
occupied by EICs and Nabobs. With a pamphlet
written for Mohamed Ali Chan, he scattered
all the nouveaux riches in London.

                              To my surprise,
I find I rather like him,
this child of the Macpherson clan
who came to be MP from Camelford and drive
a private coach, though it's true
I cannot read his book for very long.
Who can say what spoke to him
in Ruthven, tiny village on the Highland Road
near Perth where plowmen unearthed shards
of Roman bowls & where the farmers
scratched St Kattan's name as *Chattan*
on the Druid stones. Here he saw
an end that emptied the entire north
of ancient feeling. The broken clansmen
staggered to his very door. It was
the Highland Army's last assembly; Cluny had
a price upon his head; Macphersons fled,
then hid him; Charles was somewhere
in the islands or in France. The barracks

210

where Macpherson played a soldier burned,
and he was nine. Then enormous quiet.

I close the book and walk out on the shingle
staring into low wet fog upon the Firth
that rolls against the rocks like spindrift.
The beach is empty, save for one old man
and one black bird that's flying toward the mine.
The limbs of trees are heavy, drip—
as if with melting snow.

                       When old men faltered
in their songs
Macpherson squared the widening empty circles
with what came to hand: with rocks,
with fogs, with dripping trees, deserted beaches
and old men by which heraldic birds
were briefly lured to perch
on names like *Fingal, Oscar, Gaul*
as if on severed limbs upon a field of slaughter
the sight of which did not appal
the rock nearby or wood and water which afforded
the clear eye a rare and charming beauty
where the Erse Nation was not furious with Lord North.
Seeking to fill emptiness, Macpherson
marked its boundaries,
surveyed & gerrymandered sentimental space—

Samuel Johnson filled that space
with rage, Napoleon with a military will.
They too longed for grander feelings; an actual object
and a cause. Heraldic birds appeared
on the horizon, flying north.
Macpherson travelled south.
The Earl of Wemyss stared happily upon his Venus
signed *Van Dyck.*

IX

And I stare quizzically at what I've written here,
at language that has used me one more time
for consequential or inconsequential ends that
are not mine. Can I tell which (& where)
by making declarations: the one? the other, now?
By speaking Edward's language
to his dear and faithful cousin, Eymar de Valance,
as a second generation speaks
the ruins of a first?

                     by finding not
in our
Sir Michael Wemyss
good word? or occupying picturesque positions
on the summit of a cliff?

Can I tell which (& whose) by calling points
that mark the intersection of some arbitrary boundaries
castle, queen, and *mine?*
boundaries of a space by no means empty
where the cost of lodging
is exacted by a pile of books, by *castle, queen,* and *mine,*
attainted absent lord, and black heraldic bird?
I close the book and walk out on the shingle
staring into low wet fog, etcetera.
I never closed the book. I never left the room
to walk along the beach.

                   Tourist? Paying guest—
of language of
the place, but heading further north
and pledging silence.

I've heard a scholar filled his empty life
by tracing down a thousand plagiaries from eighty
sources in MacP. I've heard the casket letters
occupied a thousand scholars who had emptiness to fill

for half a thousand years. Otherwise,
who knows, they might have filled those spaces
with the motions of a Bothwell or a Cumberland
through whom the language of the place
spoke itself to consequence.

I've heard a man found Waverley "so colourless
and unconvincing as to be
a virtual
                    gap on the page."

And where are you, Kirkpatrick?   (& Matthias)

Or you—
              whose little ship ran battle-scarred
before the wind to Norway, piloted
by Hanseatic sailors well past lowland Karmoi.
Did you follow then the rocky coast to Bergen?
and from there a black heraldic bird
to Copenhagen, Malmö? Did you sail north from Orkney
shouting into gales, spoken for by oaths,
language howling you to silence deep as Dragsholm?
Did she say, whose French was not
Brantôme's, whose verse appalled Ronsard,
l'oiseau sortira de sa cage? And did she say, before
Kirkcaldy chased you through the mists
around the Orkneys, *Sonnets in italic hand
conjure you to Scania....*
*You'll crawl in squalid circles for eleven years & more
widdershins
and widdershins, weeping....*

So Bothwell's route is mine. I'll stuff my mouth
with herring, think of Anna Throndsen,
and not return to Fife either with the Maid of Norway
or the Duke of Orkney's head.
My bird of Sentiment took flight from Inverness.
Tangent to our Baltic steamer's course, he's plighted

to a Hanseatic taxidermist who will stuff him
for an øre—

              Or: *l'oiseau sortira de sa cage?*

Old Bert Brecht, wily exile,
fleeing just ahead
of the Gestapo,
making for L.A. by way of Finland,
did you really see "High up in Lapland
towards the polar arctic sea,
a smallish hidden door"?

Through that door *black wings, yellow beak
round eyes...*

                    appear a moment, pause

                       & disappear

NOTES

One takes what one needs, but with thanks and praise. I am indebted to an odd assortment of books and authors for facts, fancies, passages of verse or of prose, translations, information, scholarship and scandal which I have had occasion in these poems to quote, plagiarize, wilfully ignore, tactfully modify, stupidly misconstrue, or intentionally travesty. I have plundered these sources (1) to get my general bearings in the course of a composition or (2) for passages and fragments which provide documentary material in which poetic energy can be isolated so as to expand the voicing of particular parts of this book. The debts acknowledged below constitute a poet's often random, pretty unscholarly (though sometimes purposeful) reading over certain periods of time when engaged in assembling certain kinds of structures.

Part 1: Jules Michelet, *Satanism and Witchcraft* ("Renaissance"). Julio Caro Baroja, *The World of the Witches* in the Glendinning translation, from which several phrases are quoted & paraphrased ("An Absence"). John Read, *Prelude to Chemistry*; Frederic Spiegleberg, *Alchemy as a Way of Salvation*; C.G. Jung, "The Idea of Redemption in Alchemy" ("Five Lyrics from 'Poem in Three Parts'").

Part 2: W.H. Auden, *Secondary Worlds*; Robert Duncan, Introduction to *Bending the Bow*; Sylvia Plath, *The Bell Jar*; A. Alvarez, *The Savage God* ("Part of an Answer"). Nadezhda Mandelstam, *Hope Against Hope*, John Garvick, his great but so far untranscribed oral masterpiece; tags from Yeats, Joyce, de Sade, Octavio Paz, Marianne Moore, Jean Cocteau ("For John, After His Visit: Suffolk, Fall"). F.S. Howes, *The English Musical Renaissance* ("Once for English Music"). Edmund Wilson, *To the Finland Station* ("Three Around a Revolution" and "Bakunin in Italy"). Kurt Seligmann, *A History of Magic* ("Six for Michael Anania"). Paul Hindemith, *Libretto: Matis der Maler*; Otto Benesch, *The Art of the Renaissance in Northern Europe*, chapter II; Ian Kemp, *Hindemith*; F.W. Sternfeld, ed., *Music in the Modern Age*, chapter 2: "Germany", Elaine Padmore; Norman Cohn, *The Pursuit of the Millennium* ("Double Sonnet on the Absence of Text: 'Symphony Matis der Maler', Berlin, 1934:—Metamorphoses"). Thomas Hardy, *Jude the Obscure*; H.T. Lowe Porter, translator's note, *Dr Faustus*; A.F.E. Burroughs, *West Midland Dialects of the Fourteenth Century*; J. Matthias, *Bucyrus* and "Th' Entencioun and Speche of Philosophres"; tags from King Alfred, Chaucer, Langland, John of Mandeville, Wycliffe, the *Pearl* poet, Joseph of Arimathaea; George Steiner, *Language and Silence* ("Turns"). *The Great Tournament Roll of Westminster, A Collotype Repro-*

duction of the Manuscript: Sydney Anglo's Historical Introduction, Appendices I and II—Tiptoft's Ordinances and the Revels Account of Richard Gibson, and the Analytical Description; Gordon Donaldson, *Scottish Kings*; Lt. Colonel Howard Green, *Battlefields of Britain and Ireland*; Peter Alexander, Introduction to Shakespeare's (?) *Henry VIII* in the *Collins Tudor Shakespeare* ("Double Derivation, Association, & Cliché: from *The Great Tournament Roll of Westminster*"). Tacitus, *The Annals of Imperial Rome*, chapters 10 and 11; Stephen Gosson, *School of Abuse*; R.R. Clarke, *East Anglia*, chapters 6 and 7; I.A. Richmond, *Roman Britain*, chapters 1, 2, and 5; Donald R. Dudley and Graham Webster, *The Rebellion of Boudicca*; Patrick Crampton, *Stonehenge of the Kings*, chapter 1; Ronald Blythe, ed., *An Aldeburgh Anthology* ("East Anglian Poem" and "Epilogue from a New Home").

Part 3: C.J. Stranks, *St Etheldreda: Queen and Abbess*; *The Book of Margery Kempe* (translated by W. Butler-Bowdon with an introduction by R.W. Chambers); Julian of Norwich, *Revelations of Divine Love* (in the Clifton Wolters translation); P. Franklin Chambers, *Juliana of Norwich: an Introductory Appreciation and an Interpretive Anthology* ("Two Ladies" and "59 Lines Assembled Quickly Sitting on a Wall Near the Reconstruction of the Lady Juliana's Cell"). Justin Kaplan, *Mr Clemens and Mark Twain*; Mark Twain, "The Celebrated Jumping Frog of Calavaras County" ("Mark Twain in the Fens"). Joanna Richardson, *Verlaine*; Enid Starkie, *Arthur Rimbaud*; Paul Verlaine, *Sagesse* ("Paul Verlaine in Lincolnshire"). W.G. Arnott, *Orwell Estuary*; George Ewart Evans, *Ask the Fellows who Cut the Hay*; Julia Pipe, *Port on the Alde*; Rudyard Kipling, "A Smuggler's Song" ("Lines for the Gentlemen"). Julian Tennyson, *Suffolk Scene* ("Brandon, Breckland: The Flint Knappers"). R.A. Edwards, *The Fighting Bishop*; R.B. Dobson, ed., *The Peasants' Revolt of 1381*; Rodney Hilton, *Bond Men Made Free*; Norman Cohn, *The Pursuit of the Millennium* ("26 June 1381/1977"). Johan Huizinga, *Homo Ludens*; *The Manual of Horsemanship of the British Horse Society and Pony Club*; Lars Norén, "August"; tags from John Berryman, W.B. Yeats, Robert Hass, Wordsworth, *King Lear* ("Poem for Cynouai").

Part 4: Gunnar Ekelöf, "Xoanon" from *Selected Poems* translated by W.H. Auden and Leif Sjöberg with an Introduction by Göran Printz-Påhlson ("After Ekelöf"). Lars Norén, "Augusti" from *Viltspeglar* ("August"). Göran Sonnevi, "Tomrum som faller…" from *Ingrepp-modeller* ("Void which falls out of void…"). Octavio Paz, *Salamandra* and *Ladera Este* ("Free Translation and Recombination: Fragments from Octavio Paz"). César Vallejo, "Ágape" from *Los Heraldos Negros* ("Agape"). Anon., "Propast Carstva Srpskoga", "Carica Milica I Vladeta Vojvoda" and other fragments from *The Battle of Kossovo*; Albert B. Lord, *The Singer of Tales* ("To V.V.: On Our Translation of the Kossovo Fragments"). "Kosovka Djevojka" ("The Kossovo Maiden").

Part 5: Adam Mickiewicz, *Pan Tadeusz* (in the G.R. Noyes translation); *Adam Mickiewicz* (Unesco Books: essays by several hands); V.L. Benes and N.J.G. Pounds, *Poland*; Tadeusz Ocioszynski, *Poland on the Baltic*; Jerzy Jan Lerski, *A Polish Chapter in Jacksonian America*; Henry Beston, *The St Lawrence*; Guilbert Parker and Claude G. Bryan, *Old Quebec*; Eric Zagrans, two rejected lines from an early draft of his translation into Yiddish of "The Love Song of J. Alfred Prufrock" ("The Stefan Batory Poems"). C.E. l'Ami, ed. and translator, *The Poetry of Lermontov*; Guy Daniels, ed. and translator, *A Lermontov Reader*; Mihail Lermontov, *A Hero of Our Time* (in the Nabokov translation); Janko Lavrin, *Lermontov*; Serge Sovietov, *Mickiewicz in Russia*; Edward J. Brown, *Russian Literature Since the Revolution*; Yon Barna, *Eisenstein*; Colette Shulman, ed., *We the Russians*; James H. Billington, *The Icon and the Axe*; Robert Payne, *The Fortress*; Charles M. Wiltse, *The New Nation*; R.C. McGrane, *The Panic of 1837*; N.K. Risjord, *The Old Republicans*; Sir Edward Creasey, *Fifteen Decisive Battles*; Alan Wykes, *An Eye on the Thames*; Basil E. Cracknell, *Portrait of London River*; Philip Howard, *London's River*; A.P. Herbert, *The Thames* ("The Mihail Lermontov Poems").

Part 6: Abel Gance, *Napoleon* ("At a Screening of Gance's *Napoleon*: Arts Theatre, Cambridge"). Ezra Pound, "Cino" ("E.P. in Crawfordsville"). Arthur Mizner, *The Saddest Story* ("F.M.F. from Olivet"). Sir Geoffrey Keynes, ed., *Sir Thomas Browne: Selected Writings* ("Words for Sir Thomas Browne"). François Villon, "L'Epitaphe Villon"; Mrs Thatcher on The Falklands, quoted in *Le Monde*; Neil Lands, *The French Pyrenees*; E. Cortade, *Collioure: Guide Historique et Touristique*; Yves Bonnefoy, "Jean et Jeanne"; Antonio Machado, "El sol es un globo de fuego"; Guiraud Riquièr, "Be'm degra de chantar tener..."; Stéphane Mallarmé, "Prose— pour des Esseintes" ("A Wind in Roussillon"). Sir William Fraser, *Memorials of the Family of Wemyss of Wemyss*; Göran Sonnevi, "Void which falls out of void..."; *The Gododdin*; Antonia Fraser, *Mary Queen of Scots*; Robert Gore-Browne, *Lord Bothwell and Mary Queen of Scots*; Moray McLaren, *Bonnie Prince Charlie*; John Prebble, *Culloden*; Sir Walter Scott, *Waverley*; Robert Louis Stevenson, *Kidnapped*; Jenni Calder, *Robert Louis Stevenson*; A.N. Wilson, *The Laird of Abbotsford*; Adam Smith, *The Wealth of Nations*; Fred R. Glahe, *Adam Smith and the Wealth of Nations*; R.B. Haldane, *Adam Smith*; E.W. Hirst, *Adam Smith*; John Rae, *The Life of Adam Smith*; John Fleming, *Robert Adam and His Circle*; James Macpherson, *The Poems of Ossian*; Derick S. Thomson, *The Gaelic Sources of*

MacPherson's Ossian; Bailey Saunders, *Life and Letters of James Macpherson*; Henry Mackenzie, *The Man of Feeling*; Gerard A. Barker, *Henry Mackenzie* ("Northern Summer"). Other debts—especially those to poets—are numerous but, I trust, obvious: whether in the characteristic adjective or in the full scale rite of homage.

Much of the material I have made use of in "Northern Summer", as also in the longer historical sequences from *Bucyrus*, *Turns*, and *Crossing*, is merely a matter of school history. However, the mid-Atlantic nature of some of these poems makes for a problem: it all depends on where you went to school. American readers may not recognize one set of references, British readers may not recognize another. Of course neither British nor American readers will necessarily recognize the Polish or Russian references. My publisher, after some perplexity among reviewers of my first two books, suggested more extensive notes for *Crossing*. Though I decided in the case of *Crossing*—and have decided once again—to limit the notes to a bibliography, I will add here what might be an example of "a more extensive note" to one of the shorter poems in order to suggest, if nothing else, what questions of length, expense, and ugliness are involved. Only David Jones has really mastered the art of opening up "unshared backgrounds"—or even, as one must now say, "unshared foregrounds"—in notes. The following was put together for a BBC broadcast of "26 June 1381/1977".

> Henry Despenser (or le Despenser, or Lespenser—the name is given a French pronunciation in the seventeenth line) was Bishop of Norwich during the period of the Peasants' Revolt and put down an East Anglian version of that insurrection in the fields of North Walsham on 26 June 1381. The leader of the Norfolk revolt, Geoffrey Lidster (or Litster, or Litester), a dyer by trade, was defeated, tried, and confessed by Despenser, who then followed him as he was dragged behind a wagon to the place of execution, trying to keep the condemned man's head from bouncing on the road. For putting down the revolt the Norfolk nobles gave Despenser the famous painted retable, or reredos, now in Norwich Cathedral, which was restored by Pauline Plummer in 1958. The poem has to do with the revolt, the execution of Lidster, the painting of the reredos, the restoration of the reredos, and with various reactions to these events. A fragment from one of the allegorical letters of protest which circulated during the Peasants' Revolt is quoted in the poem, as is the well-known rhyme of the period about Adam and Eve. Though in point of historical fact Despenser's brass has disappeared, we know that the epitaph included the words *miles amatus* and *boni pastoris mens*— "beloved soldier" and "the soul of this good shepherd". I should

perhaps add, by way of introduction, that malachite and azurite were used in the restoration of the anonymous Norwich master's painting of the last events in the life of Christ, and that the restorer had to replace entirely the head and arms of Christ on the cross in the wooden center panel.

Several of my oldest friends and closest readers have urged me to include a very early prose-poem from *Bucyrus*, "Statement", in this selection. Though I find myself unable to make it fit coherently into the first section of the present volume, I have decided to print it here. The quotation is from Christopher Caudwell's *The Concept of Freedom*.

STATEMENT

Once upon a time Ezra Pound, when he was still a young man, not so young he was still an imagist, but still young enough that he was a vorticist, once upon a time ol' Ez had him a friend called Gaudier-Brzeska. Now this Gaudier, this Gaudier-Brzeska who was a friend of Ezra Pound's (Pound the vorticist—always honoring craft) this Gaudier was a craftsman of genius—a sculptor. He worked on stone with his hands, and his hands were trained—*trained* hands. I mean the man knew what he did, didn't hack it with cudgels and hammers, didn't just kick it or punch it, he *sculpted* the stone with his exquisite perfectly trained controlled and controlling hands. (If, for example, the man had liked violin, he would have taken the time to find out where one puts down one's fingers. If, for example, the man had liked the cooking of pastries, he would have learned from a pastry cook how to cook pastries. If, for example, the man had liked carpentry, he would have learned that screws hold under certain kinds of stresses where nails don't—etc. etc.) But his medium was stone. And he was a craftsman of genius—*of genius*. He had learned his craft, do you follow me. And that turned out (it does turn out, if you're serious, but most people aren't) to spell the difference between freedom and slavery, or, to be more precise in the parable, between freedom and imprisonment. "The instincts are not free springs of connation towards a goal. They are, so far as they can be abstractly separated, unconscious necessities, as Kant realized. They are unfree. But in their realization as behaviour, when these innate things-in-themselves become things-for-themselves and interact with their environment (which also changes and is not the dead world of

221

physics) they also change. Above all, they are changed in human culture. As a result of this change, these necessities become conscious, become emotion and thought; they exist for themselves and are altered thereby. The change *is* the emotion or thought, and now they are no longer the instincts, for they are conscious and consciousness is not an ethereal but a material determining relationship. The necessity that is conscious is not the necessity that is unconscious. The conscious goal is different from the blind instinctive goal. It is freer." So then Gaudier. Gaudier choosing craft and consciousness, choosing freedom. So then Gaudier—Gaudier refusing to be enslaved by refusing to know, Gaudier refusing imprisonment. But they tried, the governments and their jailers, they tried, the governments and jailers unconscious and therefore unfree, to jail, in the war, this conscious spirit, this Gaudier. But Gaudier loved freedom, and because he loved freedom learned craft. Because he loved freedom learned craft so perfectly that he became a craftsman of genius. And his medium was stone. Stone were the jails of the governments and the jailers. Stone was his medium—a genius with exquisite perfectly trained controlled and controlling hands. Free hands. Free because they knew craft. Jails, Penitentiaries, Sanatoriums, all made out of stone. Stone walls, many feet thick. Stone jails. Jail-thick stone walls where they put him, craftsman and free, they—the governments making their wars.

Minutes after they threw him there in his cell, minutes after they locked him in that cage of stone, Gaudier, Pound's friend the vorticist, took, with his bare hands, an eight-foot-thick wall apart and went home.

ACQ 4755

2/9/93
gift

PS
3563
A858
N6
1984